LIVING LONG & LIVING WELL

JOHN ROSENOW
LIVING LONG & LIVING WELL

INSPIRING STORIES OF CREATING AND
CONTRIBUTING DURING THE WISDOM YEARS

WISDOM OAK
PRESS

Lincoln, Nebraska

Living Long & Living Well
Copyright © 2014 by John E. Rosenow

All rights reserved under International and Pan-American Copyright Conventions.
Published in the United States by
Wisdom Oak Press, P.O. Box 84351, Lincoln, NE 68508.

ISBN 978-0-9905544-1-7
eBook ISBN 978-0-9905544-2-4
Library of Congress Control Number 2014944977

Cover and page design by Stacy Hadley
Page layout by Adam Wagler

Lincoln, Nebraska

CONTENTS

Prologue: The Stories of our Lives — 1

Chapter 1: Frederick Law Olmsted — 5

Chapter 2: Georgia O'Keeffe — 19

Chapter 3: Joseph Campbell — 37

Chapter 4: Carl Jung — 49

Chapter 5: Wangari Maathai — 61

Chapter 6: Walt and Roy Disney — 85

Chapter 7: Margaret Mead — 109

Chapter 8: John Adams — 131

Chapter 9: Martha Graham — 155

Chapter 10: Nelson Mandela — 175

Final Thoughts: — 201
   Creating and Contributing During the Wisdom Years

End Notes — 205

Acknowledgements — 215

Prologue

THE STORIES OF OUR LIVES

I've always loved stories. My favorite childhood memories include my family's Saturday-morning trips to the library in the little Nebraska town near our farm. The patient lady who served as the librarian—perhaps a Saturday volunteer—seemed to know what I liked, and always pointed out biographies written specifically for youngsters. The books I remember were intentionally uplifting stories, often about the lives of precocious kids who grew up to become famous people. Most of the books' content was about their young lives, and the closing chapter was always about something famous they did as an adult.

I still remember a story from the life of Luther Burbank, the prolific plant breeder. Burbank wanted to popularize a lovely white lily which unfortunately stank to high heaven. Burbank planted fields of them in the hopes that nature, in her varied abundance, would spin off an oddball, one without the nasty smell. One day, Burbank was about to inspect a big field of his lilies when he actually detected a hint of a pleasant fragrance in the air. He crawled on his hands and knees from flower to flower until he found the one with the wonderful smell. According to the story, Burbank ripped of a piece of his shirt to mark the plant so he could come back and find it again in the big field. The propagation of that one plant, over and over, made it possible for countless people to annually enjoy sweet-smelling Easter Lilies.

The authors of those books wanted to encourage youthful ambition, and they did so by telling how those lives turned out. They also wanted the readers to keep reading, so they put the most inspiring part in the last chapters.

As a young boy, I was a constant frustration for my parents because I just had to watch the end of the TV show before coming to dinner. Also, from time-to-time as a child I would have "story" dreams, some or another adventure based on whatever my young head was full of at the time. If I woke up in the middle of one of those dreams, I developed the knack for going back to sleep and dreaming the rest of the story. I had to know how things turned out.

Those books about the early experiences of people who made meaningful contributions during their lives turned out to provide a helpful mindset for my career. I was fortunate to be at the right place at the right time to be able to start the Arbor Day Foundation when I was 21. As the Foundation's long-time chief executive, and I was blessed to make a career of inspiring people to plant trees to improve their neighborhoods and communities, and restore national forests and rain forests--as well as supporting people who are working together to make life better for the people in their communities and for future generations. Through the years I have found practical guidance and continual inspiration from reading countless biographies and histories.

However my past reading wasn't especially relevant for obtaining insights as I look ahead to seek ways to creatively contribute during my approaching Wisdom Years.

The developmental psychologist Erik Erikson, as he outlined the eight stages of the human life cycle, generously labeled the eighth stage the Wisdom Years, considered to begin at around age 65. According to Erikson the positive characteristics of this life stage can include accumulated knowledge, inclusive understanding, and mature judgment.

As I look toward the last chapters of my life, I want the most inspiring parts to be toward the end. Looking for models, my biography-reading became more intentional. I read about many people who made important contributions during their Wisdom Years in arenas that I especially care about: improving the environment, supporting people's personal and spiritual growth, creating a well-functioning society. As I read and researched, it occurred to me that many other people are looking for the last chapters of their lives to be the most rewarding as well. So my personal quest began to take shape as this book. On my journey of understanding, I found some amazing stories.

Actually, though, we should not be so amazed. In his mega-bestseller, *Outliers: The Story of Success*, Malcolm Gladwell delves into many factors that explain some people's seemingly extraordinary accomplishments. One applies directly to the big story of this book. So many exceptional achievers--people in athletics or business or technology or the arts—were simply the ones who had practiced 10,000 hours. Gladwell reports on numerous studies in diverse fields which analyzed the differences between the elite and the merely good, the high-level contributors and the rest. Again and again, the difference came down to practice, even more than raw talent, specifically the 10,000 hours of practice which seems to be the magic number needed to become an expert.

Gladwell tells of well-known people such as Bill Gates, Mozart, and the Beatles who enjoyed extraordinary circumstances and accumulated their 10,000 hours of practice at a young age. But a person's chances of accumulating those 10,000 hours of practice obviously increase by the time they reach their Wisdom Years. For many, it just takes a while to become an expert.

Beyond experience, beyond the hours and hours of practice, there's an aspect that I suppose is simply the human spirit. In a way that some would say is contrary to common sense, contrary to self-interest, many people in their Wisdom Years, more than at any other stage in their life, look to the future, to the legacy they will leave. One might think that when we're younger we would care more about the future; that's where we'll live the rest of our long lives. But again and again, as you'll see in the following pages, we find the desire to make a lasting contribution, and the ability to do so creatively, can come to fullest bloom during the Wisdom Years.

Often, thankfully, that's how things turn out.

Chapter One

FREDERICK LAW OLMSTED

A democratic development of the highest significance.

Perhaps never in all of history had there been such a one-man crusade against ugly boats.

As he led the landscape architecture team for the 1893 World's Columbian Exposition—The Chicago World's Fair—Frederick Law Olmsted had countless details to oversee. The site he had recommended beside Lake Michigan had been selected, and Olmsted had drawn the master plan which laid out the locations for the small lakes to be dredged into existence to set off the gleaming white buildings to be built. In three short years a showplace was to be brought forth from a sandy patch of desolate scrub land, a magic city that was to host the world

At one time there were nearly 20,000 workers on the 600-acre grounds, constructing the huge Beaux Arts buildings, and installing Olmsted's landscaping. With way too little available time, the landscaping crews furiously planted hundreds of thousands of trees, shrubs, ferns, and aquatic plants; established massive lawns; even sourced, tended, and introduced thousands of ducks, pigeons, and exotic birds. Olmsted was a busy guy.

Olmsted was 70 years old as the Chicago Exposition neared completion. He had behind him a long and distinguished career that included the creation of many great and sublime parks throughout the United States, including New York City's incomparable Central Park. He was the creator and champion of the profession of landscape architecture. He had nothing to prove personally, and he was dealing with a horrific toothache, roaring ringing in his ears, and insomnia. And he had all of those bushes to plant.

Yet he made the time and fought the battles that were needed to insure that it would be elegant little boats that plied the waters of the lakes that his crews had created.

Olmsted's whole life—his purposeful travels, his keen observation, his 10,000 hours of experience—had taught him that the scenery as a whole was the thing… that everything the visitors would see matters. He was determined that exposition guests would not be subjected to unsightly steam-powered tugboats coughing up smoke as they loudly chugged across the waterways.

Tugboats represented the conventional wisdom, the "efficient" way to transport people, and Daniel Burnham, the architect who led the exposition project, seemed ready to accept a proposal from a tugboat manufacturer who made a strong case for their practically.

Olmsted was steadfast, insisting as often and as firmly as necessary that boats of an elegant design be selected. He knew that all the large and small details that would make up the visual landscape were vital, and his experience taught him the importance of his vision of little boats quietly gliding across the still waters by the great buildings.

In the end, Burnham awarded the boat concession to a company which produced a lovely electric vessel of exactly the character that Olmsted wanted. The "poetic mystery" of Olmsted's vision was manifest.

THE FATHER OF LANDSCAPE ARCHITECTURE

As a child, little Fred loved to wander in the woods. Just a few short years after Olmsted's birth in 1822, his father, John Olmsted, a well-to-do dry goods merchant, sent Fred away from their comfortable city home through most of his childhood to be taught by a schoolmaster-minister in a rural village in Connecticut.

The instruction he received, such as it was, was casual at best, taught in a way that didn't engage Fred's curiosity or his intellect, and he spent all of the time he could exploring the woods. Back with his family in Hartford he would get lost in books as fervently as he had in the woods. Two of Olmsted's life-long skills—using words and designing nature with effect—had early roots.

Olmsted's eclectic career, in hindsight, offered a smorgasbord of experiences that would combine to create the unique portfolio of expertise that would make it possible for him to become America's master park builder—with a few oddballs thrown in to make life rich and interesting.

He was a sailor in the China trade. His father bought him a farm on Long Island where he learned to direct laborers and to make things grow in rocky fields. He toured Europe, observed picturesque countrysides and expansive urban parks, and wrote a travelogue, *Walks and Talks of an American Farmer in England*. The book launched his many successful writing ventures, including serving as a correspondent for the New York Times, editing magazines, and writing several books including *Cotton Kingdom: A Traveler's Observations on Cotton and Slavery in the American Slave States.* Olmsted absorbed all as he traveled; he thought a person owed it to himself to look and to feel. He learned to write about his observations and his ideas in a compelling way.

At the age of 35 Olmsted was hired as the superintendant of what was to become New York City's Central Park. When Olmsted first saw the rugged, treeless place, its future magnificence was less than obvious: "The low grounds were steeped in the overflow and mush of pig-sties, slaughterhouses, and bone-boiling works, and the stench was sickening."[1]

The Board of Commissioners of Central Park offered prizes for the best designs for the park, and Olmsted and his friend Calvert Vaux collaborated on a design, called Greensward, which was chosen by the board to implement.[2]

Olmsted considered the park part and parcel of his commitment to social justice. He described it as "a democratic development of the highest significance."

Olmsted then began the real work of bossing men and horses, and battling budgets and bureaucrats, to raise his vision out of the rocky soil. In design and operation the park incorporated many innovations, from the ingenious traverse roads which cut below pedestrian paths to the idea of Park Keepers rather than city police.

He had made himself the country's foremost expert on parks, and he was conscious that he was founding an American profession.

Adding depth and breadth to his experience, during the Civil War Olmsted served as head of the United States Sanitary Commission, the forerunner of the Red Cross. Following his service in the war he headed a mining company in California. There he lobbied for legislation to set aside the matchless Yosemite Valley "for public use, resort, and recreation for all time."[3] The bill was passed by Congress and signed by President Lincoln.

Although Yosemite was carved out of the federal public domain, it was assigned to the state of California to manage as a park, an experiment that did not go well. Olmsted was named to head a commission to create a management plan for the park, which required that he grapple with a different situation than he had experienced in the settled East or long-settled Europe—how to manage a large wild park. He was thinking through a philosophy of preservation. "The first point to keep in mind," he wrote, "is the preservation and maintenance as exactly as possible of the natural scenery."[4] His ideas became the foundation of what eventually became Yosemite National Park, and America's national park system.

In 1865 Olmsted moved back to the east coast, resuming an on-and-off role in New York City with Central Park and other parks, and launching his landscape architecture firm which designed magnificent spaces throughout the nation—from Boston parks to the campus of Stanford University to the grounds of the United States Capitol.

1893 WORLD'S COLUMBIAN EXPOSITION— THE CHICAGO WORLD'S FAIR

One Frederick Law Olmsted project during his Wisdom Years was to have large and lasting impact—the Chicago Exposition—even though the event itself was a one-season event.

Today it's hard to imagine the typical conditions of our nation's larger cities in the late 1800s: squat, ugly buildings cramped side by side; streets that reeked of horse manure; skies darkened by coal smoke. Thomas Edison had recently invented the light bulb, but it had not been brought to wide use. Big American cities were dark and dank and dangerous. The designers of the Chicago Exposition had the intention of holding up a vision of what American civilization might achieve.

After Chicago won the vote in Congress as the city

to host the exposition, the Chicago firm of Burnham and Root was given the contract to oversee the exposition's design and construction. The firm wooed the nation's leading architects to help design the exposition's many giant buildings. Daniel Burnham recruited Frederick Law Olmsted to be the landscape architect.

Olmsted accepted the assignment for his already-busy firm because he saw the exposition as an unparalleled opportunity to bring visibility and credibility to the profession of landscape architecture. He was 68 as the work began.

After a frustrating delay, the exposition location was nailed down. At Olmsted's insistence, the site, now Jackson Park south of the city, took advantage of Chicago's outstanding natural feature, Lake Michigan. Olmsted immediately went to work on the master plan for the exposition. The plan called for dredging small lakes and canals on the sandy site, and creating elevated building sites for the exposition's massive structures.

Olmsted believed in designing and managing the entire visual effect of the exposition. He wanted everything the visitors would see to be of a piece, what he called his "poetic-mystery" objective. Everything mattered: the magnificent buildings that the superstar architects were designing, of course, but also the trees and flowers, the positioning of the buildings relative to the cobalt-blue Lake Michigan and the newly dredged waterways, the subtle arrangement of cattails and ferns and bushes and tall grasses, the great lawns to be planted—and as we know, the quiet and "becoming" boats that he wished to silently glide across the lakes and along the canals.

As a result of Olmsted's years of close and careful observation of gardens and parks throughout the United States and Europe he had learned to avoid garish displays of color. He sought subtle effects with his plantings, a gifted artist's combination of light and shadow, of graceful lines, of just the right amount of color showing through. He sought to bring the best of what he had observed in nature to this magical city, visual ideas from the parks and forests and farms and fields of Europe and America. He was not about to have gaudy groupings of showy roses assaulting the visitor. He wanted people to look more deeply to see the beauty of the landscape as a whole, how things quietly fit together. He even cared about the smells, planting honeysuckle and summersweet near places visitors would pause to enjoy the views.

To guide his team, and others working on the exposition, Olmsted wrote a ten-page memorandum which was a summary of everything he had learned through his long career about the art of landscape architecture. It wasn't just a plan, it was a way of thinking about the kinds of effects great design can have on the hearts and minds of those it serves.

But before these elegant scenes could be brought forth from the scrubby, sandy soil, there were a thousand details to manage: plans to be drawn, lakes and canals to be dredged with horse teams, elevated building sites to be laid out using the same horse power, plants to be sourced, shipped or grown, and ultimately planted. Manure had to be spread to enrich the soil—one thousand carloads from the Union Stock Yards, two thousand more from the horses working on the site.

At times during the three years of the exposition's construction, Olmsted was exhausted, once seeking respite in a European trip to try to restore his health. At times he worked with the energy of a man a third his age.

Then as now, commercial and political interests pressed Olmsted and Burnham to compromise their vision. Buffalo Bill Cody's Wild West Show was rejected as an exhibitor as incompatible with the exposition's theme. (Cody arranged for space right outside the exposition grounds. His show made a fortune.)

One element of Olmsted's plan that he worked diligently to maintain was a building-free Wooded Island. As a counterpoint to the gleaming-white neoclassical buildings that sprang forth at the exposition, the Wooded Island was to be its landscape centerpiece. Cattails were to be planted on the banks of the island, as well as ferns and sedges, with flowers peeking through in an unobtrusive way.

Envisioning a landscape that was both graceful and beautiful came naturally to Olmsted, as did beating back ideas that would compromise the result he was after. Some of the proposals for the Wooded Island were not bad ideas, but he knew they just didn't fit there: a Chicago symphony music hall, an Indian exhibit, the ethnology chief's exotic villages. Olmsted even successfully negotiated no less a personality than Theodore Roosevelt off the island. Roosevelt, then head of the U.S. Civil Service Commission, agreed to a smaller island as the location for the hunting camp exhibit of his Boone and Crockett Club. Olmsted finally agreed to a low-profile exhibit of Japanese temples tucked amongst the trees on the island. Wooded Island remained wooded, a calm green counterpoint in the landscape.

Personal and professional tragedy did not stop Olmsted. When the firm's twenty-nine-year-old on-site superintendant, Harry Codman, died unexpectedly following an appendectomy, Olmsted took over the direct supervision of the exhibition's landscaping work himself.

The last-minute installation of the landscaping for the complex construction project was as challenging as one might expect. The grounds were used for staging construction materials for the massive buildings later than had been scheduled. There was a desperate shortage of plants as shipments failed to arrive and some early plantings failed to survive. During planting season, torrential rains soaked the already-saturated soil. Through it all, Olmsted's crews worked day and night to do what they could.

Thousands of people worked through the night before opening day, cleaning up debris, scrubbing and cleaning and painting, planting flowers and laying sod. Opening day itself was headlined by President Grover Cleveland, a descendant of Christopher Columbus, and shared by half a million visitors. The crowds found glorious bright-white buildings, great lawns and artistic plantings, and ponds graced by ducks, egrets and, to Olmsted's relief, elegant electric boats.

Attendance started slowly in the spring of the exhibition's season, below the planners' projections, and below their budget. But the word of the exposition's grandeur spread, by its many visitors and by awe-struck newspaper reporters, to small towns and big cities across the nation. By the end of the show in October, millions of people had been through the gates, and many million more had been inspired by the photographs they had seen and the stories they had heard.

Those millions included town-builders and planners and authors and developers. Even the workers were affected, including a carpenter named Elias Disney who told stories of this great city for visitors to his son Walt.

At an 1893 gathering of the artists of the exposition, their leader, Daniel Burnham, was presented with a giant silver loving cup. In his acceptance remarks, Burnham recognized Olmsted's crucial contributions: "In the highest sense he is the planner of the Exposition—Frederick Law Olmsted. An artist, he paints with lakes and wooded slopes; with lawns and banks and forest-covered hills; with mountain-sides and ocean views. He should stand where I do tonight, not for his deeds of later years alone, but for what his brain has wrought and his pen has taught for half a century."[5]

During his Wisdom Years, with his fellow designers and visionaries, Olmsted helped teach the great lesson of his life—that American cities can be beautiful…true inspirations for the human spirit.

THE BILTMORE ESTATE

The Wisdom Years can offer opportunities to make a difference in ways we may never know—the case of the other great Olmsted passion during these years: George Vanderbilt's Biltmore Estate near Asheville, North Carolina.

A large part of the work that Olmsted personally performed was along the lines of what he had done elsewhere—landscaping the grounds of a wealthy patron's private estate. But at Biltmore he had a large canvas upon which to paint, acres and acres of natural forest in the Blue Ridge Mountains with a magnificent view of the distinctive peaks of Mount Pisgah in the distance.

On the estate, Olmsted practiced his craft with zest and effect. He worked with the architect to locate the French chateau that was to become Biltmore House to embrace the full view of Mount Pisgah. As roads were sited, he decreed that they were to wind around established beech, black gum, sweet gum, sourwood, chestnut and hickory trees so that the trees would not be removed for construction. He designed gardens and arboretums, thoughtfully positioned the greenhouse and adjacencies, and created a park surrounding Biltmore—all in the finest tradition of fancy country estates in England and America.

However Olmsted's great and lasting contribution at Biltmore was the management of the estate's thousands of acres of forest.

When George Vanderbilt purchased his forest, he had only the vaguest idea as to what he would do with it. "Make a park of it, I suppose,"[6] he told Olmsted. In Olmsted's purposeful travels in Europe, he had seen a number of large wooded estates managed as hunting parks, playgrounds for their wealthy owners and their friends. He had also seen some managed as sustainable forests, the trees selectively harvested for timber, replanted, thinned as needed, and harvested again. The process was repeated decade after decade, century after century. Truly sustainable forestry.

Up until that time, American farmers and timber companies had viewed forests as obstacles to settlement, or as a one-time commodity to be exploited, like mining coal. Cut and run was the rule, leaving behind debris and sometimes dreadful fires which destroyed living forests as well.

Olmsted's keen eye saw that Vanderbilt's woodland was a mixture of noble mature trees, especially in the higher elevations, and miserable new growth in areas which had been cleared by the original settlers. He candidly told Vanderbilt that the topography made a poor place for a park. But it was a superb opportunity to manage as a forest with a view to crops of timber—a fine and dignified business for an eminent capitalist like Vanderbilt. It would also present the first opportunity in America to demonstrate systematic forestry on a large scale. To lead the enterprise Olmsted needed a forester.

As luck would have it, superb luck as it turned out, at the time there was only one trained forester in

America, a strong-willed young man named Gifford Pinchot. The son of well-to-do parents, Gifford Pinchot could have chosen any number of genteel professions, but he was a man with a mission. Pinchot had studied the management of forests in France and Germany. He returned from Europe filled with the idea of managing America's great forests. Pinchot desperately needed a place to demonstrate this idea that was so novel to the nation. Olmsted's call to serve was the answer to his prayers. "I shall be delighted to take advantage of it,"[7] Pinchot replied.

Olmsted gave the young Pinchot freedom to practice his profession. As Pinchot later wrote, "It was Mr. Olmsted who was responsible for the plan to make Biltmore Estate the nest egg for practical Forestry in the United States….Here was my chance. Biltmore could be made to prove what America did not yet understand, that trees could be cut and the forest preserved at one and the same time. I was eager, confident, and happy as a clam at high tide….Mr. Olmsted took my profession seriously, and took with equal seriousness the assumption which he made that I was able to practice it. I have never forgotten what it meant to a youngster just getting started to be treated to some extent as an equal."[8]

Gifford Pinchot went on to become the founding Chief of the U.S. Forest Service. In that position he helped his friend, President Theodore Roosevelt, establish the backbone of America's national forest system. The Biltmore estate is acknowledged as America's Cradle of Forestry. The forest became Pisgah National Forest, America's first national forest.

Today national forests are among America's national treasures. In 40 states, 155 national forests—some 300,000 square miles of renewable natural resources—have been placed under professional, sustainable management…for the public good.

Ralph Waldo Emerson said, "The creation of a thousand forests is in one acorn."

Frederick Law Olmsted helped plant the acorn of America's national forests at Biltmore—during his Wisdom Years.

AUTHOR'S NOTES

A long and well-lived life is an opportunity to gain information and inspiration, especially how to be engaged and productive well into our Wisdom Years. There are always lessons to be learned if we pay attention. At the end of each chapter I'll offer a brief commentary on what struck me about each of these people, my lessons learned. No doubt you'll have your own.

These are my reactions to the life of Frederick Law Olmsted:

- *I can't help but think what a loss it would have been if Olmsted had retired before his Wisdom Years. During that vital stage of his life, Olmsted championed ideas that much of our society now takes for granted (although vigilance by citizens and by our leaders is constantly required): That our cities can—and should—be green and beautiful. That forests ought to be sustainably managed to provide wood products, beauty, and recreation opportunities; conserve wildlife and watersheds; and protect the land...for the public good.*

- *As a child, little Fred spent hours and hours on his own, roaming the woods, connecting with the natural world. Such early emotional connections with nature have been shown to be decisive in inspiring people to become conservation professionals or citizen environmental advocates as adults. However, "free-range" childhoods with lots of time roaming natural areas, away from adults, are a thing of the past. Now adults need to be purposeful in providing those nature connections for children. How can you help the children in your life connect with nature?*

- *Olmsted made things happen that just would not have been possible if he had not had his 10,000 hours of experience to become an expert.*

- *He didn't let health challenges end his career. Before and during his Wisdom Years he had to take time away from his work to recover his health. But he viewed those issues as challenges to work through, not reasons to be permanently sidelined.*

● *During his Wisdom Years he was an innovator, the opposite of the unthinking description often given people during this life stage—that they are stuck in the past. He was often doing new things in new ways; he was all about the future.*

● *Along those lines, he actively mentored promising young people. Gifford Pinchot was a sterling example. He also championed young architects in his own firm, including a female designer named Elizabeth Bullard. He supported Bullard in becoming the city landscape advisor of Bridgeport, Connecticut at a time when it was difficult to champion a woman in any profession. The city commission followed his recommendation even though landscape architecture was then basically an all-male profession. Olmsted subsequently recommended Miss Bullard for design work at the Chicago exposition. By our Wisdom Years we've often developed the strength of heart to go against the grain. It's never too late to fight prejudice.*

● *I was obviously taken by his passion for fighting ugly boats.*

● *While Frederick Law Olmsted led a large life, his story offers lessons for us all. During our Wisdom Years—no matter what our vocation or our avocation—we can find ways to pass along the insights learned from our experience, whether or not it totals 10,000 hours. We can take positive steps to address the prejudices that remain an all-too-common part of every-day life, even by doing something as simple as offering a contrary comment when prejudice is voiced. We can work to bring beauty to wherever we live, combating whatever our equivalent is to ugly boats. We can look to the future, to the legacy we leave.*

Chapter Two

GEORGIA O'KEEFFE

I get out my work and have a show for myself before I have it publically. I make up my own mind about it how good or bad or indifferent it is. After that the critics can write what they please. I have already settled it for myself so flattery and criticism go down the same drain and I am quite fine.

Although she chafed at the implied constrictions of the label, Georgia O'Keeffe was a celebrated woman artist—to many *the* great woman artist—before it was OK for a woman to be a great artist.

O'Keeffe was born in 1887 on a dairy farm near Sun Prairie, Wisconsin, and grew into womanhood before women had the right to vote, at a time when higher education was commonly considered superfluous for women, even in educated families, and many universities did not accept women anyway. Like most professions, professional artists were men, and that's the way it was.

Georgia didn't get the memo.

In 1970, when O'Keeffe was 83, the Whitney Museum of American Art mounted a career retrospective of her work. The reaction of Barbara Rose reflected those of her fellow critics:

> These days it is fashionable to believe that we have already an accurate picture of the quality art of the 1960s. The idea that any important work is

unknown to us seems out of the question. Yet there exists a body of work done during the decade of the 1960s, almost unknown to the general art public, which I believe will endure when the media favorites of today have long faded. I am speaking of the recent paintings of Georgia O'Keeffe which rounded out her recent Whitney Museum retrospective.[1]

As critical praise was heaped upon O'Keeffe and the Whitney retrospective, it set in motion what Charles C. Eldredge, former director of the National Museum of American Art, called "the O'Keeffe phenomenon, the artist's long and golden autumn, perhaps without precedent in our history."[2]

The works on display portrayed the sweep of her career and the range of her artistic expression. The show included her early charcoal, watercolor, and oil abstractions—swirls in black and white, florescent Art Nouveau flowing lines, the suggestive and the aberrant: vividly colored landscapes, many abstract, that ranged from Lake George, New York, to her beloved New Mexico; realistic yet surrealistic cow skulls that floated magically above mountains, sometimes accented by a colorful flower hovering alongside; the skyscrapers outside her window and down the street in New York City—bold and blocky black and whites that said *Metropolis*; a full-wall mural of puffy clouds from above; cornstalks and clamshells; and of course her iconic sensual flowers. "Things in my head that are not like what anyone had taught me,"[3] she called them.

In 1970 feminism was on the rise, and O'Keeffe's one-of-a-kind, I'll-do-it-my-way lifestyle fleshed out the story behind the striking paintings. Overnight she became known in a deeper way, becoming even more famous than before. Feminists worshiped her. Her increased fame followed her for the remaining 15 years of her life.

HER EARLY YEARS

As with so many people who come to renown, Georgia's station in life when she was born would not have suggested her ultimate success.

Her parents Ida and Frank were reasonably well-to-do by the standards of farm families of the time, which isn't saying much. Ida and Frank's marriage was considered by some a way to assemble a sufficiently large piece of farm ground so the family could earn a living.

Her father Frank was hard-working, kind and generous—the gentle one of the couple. Ida was more distant from the children, all seven of them. She was especially distant from her oldest daughter, Georgia, whom Ida thought was homely and less talented than her sisters. Nonetheless, through her own special combination of intention and inattention, Ida provided the mix of experiences for Georgia in her childhood that seemed to set her up for her extraordinary life.

On one hand, Ida made sure that Georgia had drawing, painting, and music lessons. Then Ida pretty much left her alone. Georgia basically had an unsupervised childhood. She played with dolls, drew and painted to keep up with her lessons, and spent hours and hours by herself in nature. In her later years, O'Keeffe would remember her childhood as a time of freedom, the time she learned to love flowers and landscapes and extreme weather.

There is one aspect of Ida's parenting approach that today's over-eager parents would do well to emulate: While she made sure that her daughters had painting and drawing lessons, she "neither encouraged nor discouraged her daughters, thereby teaching them that their art was their own, and that they should aim for excellence only because they wanted to."[4] Georgia obviously wanted to. And her mother supported her, not with warm encouragement, but with the best education that they could afford.

During her 20s, Georgia's life reflects a principle later proscribed by physician, writer, and champion of mind/body/spiritual healing Deepak Chopra: Hold on to your vision of where you want to go, but don't get hung up on how to get there. Be alert to the opportunities that present themselves as you go.

As a child of 12, Georgia proclaimed that she was going to be an artist. In obtaining her education and launching her career, the path Georgia marched was anything but a straight line. She attended classes at the Art institute of Chicago; the Art Students League in New York City; the League's Outdoor School at Lake George, New York; the University of Virginia, Charlottesville; and Teachers College, Columbia University, New York City.

She taught at an Amarillo, Texas high school; Columbia College in Columbia, South Carolina; the University of Virginia; and West Texas State Normal College, Canyon, Texas. She began work as a commercial artist, which she found mind-numbingly dull, but an extended bout with measles provided a welcome opportunity to quit. All this while Georgia was still in her 20s.

Three things happened during her turbulent twenties that proved to be decisive in setting her career and life path. For one, there was a teacher—a showboating, silk-tunic-clad oddball named Alon Bement who helped Georgia understand the possibilities of art in a way that truly made sense to her for the first time.

What had discouraged Georgia about art in her twenties was the notion that the point of painting was to imitate reality. It was supposed to be all about the subject. Bement taught art from a different perspective, a way of thinking that he had absorbed from Arthur Wesley Dow, the dean of Fine Arts at Teachers College, Columbia University. Dow taught that true creation took place inside the frame—how the composition used positive and negative space, the way the elements related to one another in a visually satisfying way. At best a painting was far more than its subject; it was a reflection of the eye and the experience and the heart of the artist.

This was all a radical notion in 1912; in fact it was the beginning of modernism. Bement's new way of thinking about art got Georgia excited about painting again.

Bement picked up on O'Keeffe's enthusiasm, and her talent. After the class ended he asked O'Keeffe to be his teaching assistant. However in order to be eligible for the position she had to have taught in secondary school. This requirement led to a second life-changing experience. Georgia reached out to the only high school teacher she knew, Alice Peretta, who taught at the high school in Amarillo, Texas. Peretta wrangled a job at the school for O'Keeffe.

So off to the dusty, wind-swept, sun-baked, God-forsaken plains of Texas she went.

O'Keeffe loved it. She loved the extreme weather and the stark landscape. She loved teaching people who had no particular interest in art. She loved that people left her alone. She loved making do. When she began, the brand-new high school didn't yet have books or supplies. She went with what was at hand. One day a boy rode his pony to school and the pony was led inside where he became the model for the day's lesson. From Amarillo on, O'Keeffe loved landscapes that would seem barren to many; she was enchanted by their simplistic grandeur.

The third decisive experience during her turbulent twenties was meeting Alfred Stieglitz.

ALFRED STIEGLITZ

Stieglitz was a renowned photographer and a tireless art promoter. The following passages from *How Georgia Became O'Keeffe: Lessons on the Art of Living* give you a sense of the man and his influence:

> Stieglitz was a relentless, spittle-lipped monologist, commanding every room he entered. Force of nature doesn't begin to describe his personality. Even a hurricane ends, a tsunami recedes. Stieglitz was indefatigable. Every thought that entered his head needed to be verbalized. Here was a man who wrote at least fifty thousand letters, and *hand-copied each one* before mailing it, for his records. Just the thought of him makes me want to take a nap. In pictures, his big, dark eyes hold the penetrating gaze of a serial killer with a credo[5]…
>
> He single-handedly elevated photography from something akin to surveying a residential street or a new pipe to a respected art form; inaugurated the concept of the one-man (or one-women) show; understood the importance of regulating the market for an artist's work by pricing the work high and limiting inventory; and reconfirmed the suspicion the human race has harbored since Eve held the apple out to Adam: Sex sells. Stieglitz was to modern art in America what Bill Gates is to personal computing: It wouldn't exist, in the way it exists, without him.[6]

> Stieglitz was an early collector of Picasso, Matisse, and Braque, but more importantly he explained them. Through his ceaseless promotion—at his studios, through his network of influential media friends, through the avant-garde magazines he published,

through his very life—Stieglitz willed America's modern art movement into being.

Like pretty much every other art student in New York, Georgia had visited his little gallery, 291, several times, to see different shows. Unlike most others who visited 291, Stieglitz ignored the quiet, confident O'Keeffe. But he lavished a lot of attention on the other art students, especially young women such as Georgia's perky friend Anita Pollitzer.

Although they initially made no personal connection, O'Keeffe knew that Stieglitz's was the opinion that mattered. In a letter to Anita, Georgia wrote, "I believe I would rather have Stieglitz like some thing—anything I had done—than anyone else I know of."[7]

At that time, inspired by her effusive mentor, Bement, Georgia created a number of ethereal, charcoal-on-paper abstractions during a period of feverish inspiration. O'Keeffe said, "I wonder if I am a raving lunatic for trying to make these things."[8] The works contained a highly personal significance that O'Keeffe could not verbalize. "Maybe the fault is with what I am trying to say," she said, "I don't seem able to find words for it."[9]

O'Keeffe sent several of her charcoal drawings to her friend Anita Pollitzer, intending her to keep them private. Despite Georgia's admonitions, Anita shared them with Stieglitz at his studio.

"At last, a woman on paper!" was his legendary response, perhaps apocryphal. Stieglitz perceived that O'Keeffe was expressing, in a new way, something fundamentally feminine.

Georgia was both upset with her friend and thrilled that her charcoals earned the admiration of the authority she most respected. Stieglitz compounded the infraction with an unauthorized showing of the works a few months later. O'Keeffe was not happy. She was in New York studying under Professor Dow, and she angrily demanded that the show be dismantled. Stieglitz talked her down, the show continued, and a three-decade relationship began.

As a child, an adolescent, and a young woman, Georgia had selectively absorbed the things she found meaningful and used them to inform her art: the connections with nature that were an indispensible part of her life; the Art Nouveau craft movement; teachers Bement and Dow; the music she loved; even the curving shape of her violin's neck—everything that could be useful to her in expressing what went on in one woman's heart.

Now she had found in Alfred Stieglitz the man who wanted to know that heart, and the promoter who wanted to bring her work to the world. Not that their relationship was an easy one. There was the detail that when they met and fell in love Stieglitz was married. His marriage took several years to untangle, and O'Keeffe and Stieglitz finally married in 1924.

"Stieglitz would become Georgia's faithful, devoted champion," O'Keeffe biographer Karen Karbo wrote, "showing her work in his various little galleries year after year, through the Roaring Twenties, the Great Depression, the Second World War, through good productive years of staggering creativity and bad years of illness, misery, and crapola... no one on earth believed in her vision and her genius more profoundly than did Stieglitz, and because of that he was irreplaceable."[10]

WHEN IS A FLOWER JUST A FLOWER?

O'Keeffe's charcoal-only days were short-lived, ending before her marriage with Stieglitz began. In the 1920s, Georgia painted apples and pears, figs and avocados. She painted trees in bold, vibrant colors, in all degrees of abstraction—brilliant red maples and chestnuts, pink birch and pine, cottony cottonwood. Green oak leaves, brown and tan leaves, dark and lavender leaves.

And her stunning, stunning skies—some realistic enough to make you wish you were at the same lake, seeing the same sky. Some sufficiently abstract that the first-time viewer might need the title to realize those colorful wavy lines actually represented clouds.

Then there were the flowers.

As she painted flowers, O'Keeffe applied the perspective from her mentor, Professor Dow. He had encouraged the painting of flowers in his treatise, *Composition*. He advised the artist to seek "not a picture of a flower...—that can be left to the botanist—but rather an irregular pattern of lines and spaces, something far beyond the mere drawing of a flower from nature."

"Her oils of the 1920s were...faithful to the appearance of her floral subjects," Charles Eldredge, wrote, "but they never lapsed into botanical illustration, their formal concerns for color and design always remaining paramount."

This is what Professor Eldredge had to say about her flower paintings in *Georgia O'Keeffe*:

> In 1926, O'Keeffe moved from the simple profiled portraits of the calla to the striking designs discovered in enlargements of the flower's interior; her *Yellow Calla*... extracts from the blossom a decorative design of great complexity. The deep recesses of the calla, surrounded by broad, flat spathe, provided in miniature the same dichotomy between near and far, deep and flat, that later charged her Southwestern landscape and bone paintings. To dive into the recesses of the subject and yet to make the whole adhere to the flat plane of the canvas was a pictorial chal-

lenge in which the artist repeatedly delighted. The formal and decorative concerns evinced in O'Keeffe's calla lilies were at the base of her aesthetic as it evolved in the 1920s, and so too was the preoccupation with natural subjects and organic principles which she indulged in her floral enlargements.[13]

The public responses of her day, however, were a bit different, nicely summarized by the critic who wrote that her paintings were "one long, loud blast of sex…sex bulging, sex tumescent, sex deflated."[14]

Everyone lives in their time, and in the 1920s Freud was the thing. New York art critics, and Alfred Stieglitz, were true believers: They embraced Freud's pronouncements that sexual repression was the prime motivator of human behavior. Everything was about sex.

From *How Georgia Became O'Keeffe*:

> Georgia felt by turns confused, embarrassed, and enraged. The simple form inspired by the curving neck and scroll of her violin didn't escape woman-centric interpretation (it was a fetus), nor did the powder-pink and turquoise-blue arches inspired by her love of music (it was something up there in the neighborhood of the uterus). Her alligator pears, as avocados were then called, were pendulous breasts. Her stalks of corn, penises—or vaginas. It hardly mattered. It got people riled up. Between the lines of the reviews you can sense the hand of the panting critic.[15]

From time to time O'Keeffe tried to straighten out the critics. In her preface to an exhibition, she wrote, "everyone has many associations with flowers—the idea of flowers." She cited the softness of flowers, their perfume, regretting that since they're so small people seldom really study them. "So I said to myself—I'll paint what I see—what the flower is to me but I'll paint it big and they will be surprised into taking time to look at it. I will make even busy New Yorkers take time to see what I see of flowers."

She was certainly successful in making them stop and look, but she sharply disagreed with what so many lookers found there. "I made you take time to look at what I saw and when you took time to really notice my flower you hung all your own associations with flowers on my flower and you write about my flower as if I think and see what you think and see of the flower—and I don't."[16]

Whether O'Keeffe was boldly putting sexual content out there for all to see, subconsciously portraying her sensual feminine nature, or simply reflecting the forms and colors of beautiful flowers—you can decide.

BEYOND FLOWERS

In any case, her flowers and Stieglitz's ceaseless promotion made Georgia a reflection of a nascent sexual revolution and an icon of feminists. As any modern-day bookstore browser of calendars can annually observe, her flowers made her famous, to this day.

After O'Keeffe achieved renown as a result of her flamboyant abstractions and her sensual flowers, she did exactly what any Madison Avenue marketer would have told her *not* to do, and what her promoter husband loudly told her not to do—she changed her look. She decided to take up skyscrapers.

Always in tune with her environment, after Georgia moved to New York City she found herself surrounded by great big buildings—and she was fascinated by them. O'Keeffe and Stieglitz had moved to a 28th floor apartment, and the skyscrapers around them were growing to even greater heights. In painting them, she was taking on two taboos, head-on: She was deviating from a public persona that had made her famous beyond her wildest expectations, and she was painting *skyscrapers*—and skyscrapers were supposed to be painted by *men*.

Again, Georgia didn't get the memo.

The memory was vivid decades later: "The men decided they didn't want me to paint New York. They wouldn't let me [hang it]. They told me to 'leave New York to the men.' I was furious!"[17]

O'Keeffe had always arranged the paintings in Stieglitz's shows. Hers was the unerring eye that made certain each painting was hung beside the right painting, in the best light—that the total arrangement looked just so. In a group show she included one of her first skyscrapers, *New York with a Moon*, but Stieglitz had it removed. Georgia was livid, and in her solo show the following year she made sure it was included. Years later she was still celebrating when "it sold on the first day of the show: the very first picture sold. From then on they let me paint New York."[18]

She had said that one can't paint New York as it is, but rather as it is felt, and in the last half of the 1920s she set about capturing the *feeling* of Manhattan. Her paintings effused urban energy. Some were romantic images of mystery, some dark abstract patterns punctuated by light. They were dramatic and optimistic and bold.

OFF TO THE DESERT

In 1929 Georgia traveled to Santa Fe with a friend. By then she was one of America's best-known artists, the first American woman to earn her living through her art, the accomplishment a life-long dream. Her much-older husband was having an affair with an even-younger woman, and Georgia responded by leaving town. Her life was changing for good.

"I am West again and it as fine as I remembered it—maybe finer," O'Keeffe wrote her sister Catherine. "There is nothing to say about it except the fact that for me it is the only place."[19]

Through the 1930s and 1940s, O'Keeffe spent much of her time in New Mexico, staying married to and sometimes visiting and living with Stieglitz, who continued to promote her work until his death in 1946. In New Mexico, she painted and painted and painted. As always, she was struck by the landscape, captivated by its barren beauty. The dry hills and canyon cliffs, the sage brush and mesquite and cedar, the desert mesas and mountains, became her subjects. "A red hill doesn't touch everyone's heart as it touches mine and I suppose there is no reason why it should," she wrote. "You have no association with those hills—our waste land—I think our most beautiful country. You must not have seen it, so you want me always to paint flowers."[20]

Desert churches and crosses and pueblos became her subjects as well. And bones.

O'Keeffe became absolutely fascinated by the bleached bones, cattle skulls especially, that she found in the desert. She shipped barrels of them east where they decorated her New York apartment and Lake George summer home, providing constant reminders of the desert she loved.

She painted them endlessly: A cow's skull over a red, white, and blue pseudo-flag. A horse's skull gaily sporting a pink rose. A jawbone resting on a big rib. A deer skull, complete with giant anglers. Vertebrae lying on red hills, a pelvis with the moon.

Then there were the critic-puzzling floating skulls:

a ram's head levitating serenely over hills with scattered trees, accented with a hollyhock bloom with similar powers of levitation. Deer skulls with resplendent antlers hovering silently over desert mountains.

In 1938, *Life* magazine did a spread called "Georgia O'Keeffe Turns Dead Bones to Live Art." It was illustrated with four paintings and photographs of the artist. In one, O'Keeffe holds the jaw of a steer's bleached skull. The article acknowledges her "flair for collecting ordinary objects and turning them into extraordinary compositions... She looks upon skulls not in terms of death but in terms of their fine composition."[21]

While O'Keeffe had her passing fancies, passions that came and went, dry bones were not among them. She remained fascinated by the bones of animals for the rest of her long life.

HER WISDOM YEARS

I think more about tomorrow than today or yesterday.

1970 was a stellar year for the second wave of feminism in America. A U.S. Court of Appeals ruled that a company with two "substantially equal" job positions, no matter what they were called and whether or not they were "identical," fell under the Equal Pay Act, making it illegal to change the titles of positions that women held so they could be paid less. The books *Sexual Politics* and *The Female Eunuch* were published. Betty Friedan organized the Women's Strike for Equality and tens of thousands of women across the nation participated in marches. Big-hatted, strong-lunged feminist pioneer Bella Abzug was elected to Congress, famously declaring that a woman's place is in the House.

Georgia O'Keeffe didn't much care about any of that, but with her public stature renewed by the Whitney retrospective of her work, she became widely recognized as a feminist ideal: She was passionate about her independence *and* passionate about her relationships *and* passionate about her work.

She had quietly spent the prior nearly twenty of her Wisdom Years in the O'Keeffe way, doing what she wanted to do.

Georgia's lifestyle choices, based solely on what felt right to her, also set her up for the maximum likelihood of living long and living well: She exercised faithfully, she had a healthy diet, she pursued her passions. O'Keeffe loved to walk. For Georgia there was nothing like beginning the day by getting up and walking a mile—when she wasn't gardening or horseback riding. When she was seventy-four she took an eleven-day float trip with friends down the Colorado River through the Grand Canyon, taking her turn at the oars.

During her years living at Ghost Ranch in New Mexico, she grew two acres of organic fruits and vegetables so she had a continuous fresh supply. She ground her own flour for her whole-grain bread, and purchased eggs from her neighbors. She avoided processed foods and ate light, lean, and local. In her Wisdom Years, she continued to follow her painting passions, and developed a zest for travel, around the world, with her friends.

When she painted, she painted with commitment and focus. During her Wisdom Years she created a great series of paintings, *Sky Above Clouds*, depictions of what she had seen from the window of airplanes. The last of the series was the largest painting of her career. It took four days with several assistants just to stretch the twenty-four-foot-long canvas, and she spent many twelve-hour days to paint it, working top to bottom. She was seventy eight.

HER FINAL GIFT

In so many ways Georgia O'Keeffe served as a model and a heroine for the feminist movement. But she was never quite taken up by the movement itself. Her responses to the piles of letters that she answered, and the occasional visitor whom she took time to see, basically boiled down to: "Too much complaining and too little work."[22] When Gloria Steinem found her way up the dirt road to Ghost Ranch with a bouquet of red roses, unannounced, O'Keeffe didn't invite her to stay. She had things to do that day.

Georgia may have been at her most inspiring as she responded to a life change that occurred in 1971 when she was 84. One sunny day she went into a store in Abiquiu, and when she stepped back outside was surprised to find the sky had turned dark and overcast. Only the sun was still shining brightly. O'Keeffe was going blind. That was the onset of macular degeneration which left her with only peripheral vision, at best, for the rest of her life.

O'Keeffe never complained; she made the best of it. She had the walls in her home painted white to better set off the darker objects in front of them. Her watercolors were more abstract because painting them did not require her full eyesight. A young man whom O'Keeffe had hired to help around the house, Juan Hamilton, introduced her to ceramics which she could do by feel, and which others could turn into sculptures. She remained engaged in life and in the act of creation through nearly all of her 98 years. She lived long and lived well. To the end, Georgia O'Keeffe was her own woman.

AUTHOR'S NOTES

These are some of my reactions to Georgia O'Keeffe's life, a few of my lessons learned:

● *Georgia's life again confirmed the positive influence early connections with nature can have on future creativity. We saw with Olmsted how childhood hours spent in nature helped lead to his professional dedication to creatively improving the natural environment. Childhoods spent experiencing nature can be springboards to lives of other kinds of creativity as well. In the case of O'Keeffe, she developed an exquisite sensitivity to the inherent beauty of flowers and fruits, of lakes and clouds, of bleached skulls and barren landscapes. She learned to really see at an early age, a gift she retained throughout her life, even during her time of physical blindness. Making it possible for the children in our society to have enriching daily connections with nature is something each of us can seek. Environmental writer Rachel Carson said, "If I had influence with the good fairy who is supposed to preside over the christening of all children I should ask that her gift to each child in the world be a sense of wonder so indestructible that it would last throughout life." You can be that good fairy for the children in your life by helping them have enriching connections with nature.*

● *In so many ways, our habits can be decisive, and good habits can set us up for longer, happier, lives. Georgia cultivated a number of self-nurturing habits, and maintained them through her Wisdom Years: She savored loving relationships, ate healthy food in moderation, exercised regularly, spent the majority of her days doing the things she really cared about, and focused on the future, not the past. Of course these are habits that can also be first developed during the Wisdom Years, not just maintained. It's never too late to learn to nurture ourselves.*

● *Georgia was a social revolutionary through her actions, the way she lived her life. While needed change has often been led by the loud and the strident, she showed another way that can also be fruitful, and often more lasting—less complaining and more work.*

●*I especially appreciated O'Keeffe's self-honoring choice, made again and again throughout her life, including during her Wisdom Years, to change her artistic styles in response to her changing passions. It's typical for a person who achieves fame with a certain form of creative expression to feel constrained by their public persona. Walt Disney, for example, felt that he could only experiment within certain parameters consistent with "the Disney way." Georgia felt no such constraints, or at least didn't let them rule her. She followed her own star, even when her star shifted. She honored the old Rick Nelson song, "You can't please everyone, so you got to please yourself."*

Chapter Three

JOSEPH CAMPBELL

Follow your bliss and the universe will open doors for you where there were only walls.

The little boy was awe-struck by the towering totem poles, Native American gods frozen in cedar: wooden ravens with sharp beaks and six-feet-wide wing spans; fierce bears with threatening claws and fangs; wolves with long, upraised snouts; sharp-horned mountain goats and big-eyed sea animals; killer whales and dogfish sharks; supernatural sea grizzlies complete with fins. The primitive ritual masks were even stranger and more grotesque, human-animal combinations that stared at him from the walls: angry witch doctors with antler horns; ferocious tiger-shamans; scowling horned devils with little skulls atop their foreheads.

As a child, Joseph Campbell loved visiting the American Museum of Natural History in New York City with his parents. He was fascinated by the totem poles and the masks, the countless ways that primitive people tried to make sense of their place in the world, fascinated by the stories they told.

Every year he went to Buffalo Bill's Wild West Show when it came to Madison Square Garden, and he fell in love with American Indians. His supportive parents encouraged his enthusiasms by finding books about Indians that were written for young boys. He read everything he could about American Indians, and became fascinated by their myths—their traditional stories which tried to explain the origins of natural phenomena, stories that guided their behavior. He came to understood that myths were stories about the wisdom of life.

Campbell was raised as a Roman Catholic and learned to take myth seriously. He was taught to think in terms of the cycle of Christ coming into the world, teaching, dying, resurrecting, and returning to heaven. He took part in ceremonies throughout the year that immersed him in the eternal aspects of a world that constantly changes.

Campbell began to find the same motifs in the American Indians myths and what he was being taught by the nuns in church—creation, virgin births, death, resurrection. At a young age he found his lifelong mission and his passion: He had become hooked on comparative mythology.

In college, he began on the traditional academic path, working toward his doctorate. But when his university advisor pressed him to specialize, to narrow his focus, he said "to hell with it," quit his doctorate program, and retreated to a rented shack in the woods to read. For years then, and through his whole life, he read broadly—about religion, history, and anthropology; about biology, art, and philosophy. He wanted to know how humankind tried to make sense of it all, and how humans convey and institutionalize values through cultures. He wanted to figure out how it all fit together, and he wanted to share what he had learned.

Campbell's day job for 38 years was serving as a popular professor of comparative mythology at Sarah Lawrence College in New York. During those years he was a prolific writer of books about the mythologies of the world. Among his many books was *The Hero with a*

Thousand Faces, an important source of inspiration for George Lucas as he wrote and directed the Star Wars movies.

HIS WISDOM YEARS: THE POWER OF MYTH

While Campbell had become well-known to the readers of his books about mythology, his greatest opportunity to bring his lifetime of learning to a wide public audience came to him during his Wisdom Years.

When he was in his 80s, Joseph Campbell recorded a PBS series with Bill Moyers called *The Power of Myth*. Moyers was an enthusiastic Campbell reader, and a thoughtful interviewer. *The Power of Myth* series proved to be hugely popular, bringing Campbell's teachings to millions of people for the first time. Through the series, Campbell taught a broader world the lessons of his life.

Campbell was of the opinion that preachers err by trying "to talk people into belief; better they reveal the radiance of their own discovery."[1]

During his Wisdom Years, Campbell practiced what he preached throughout the interviews with Moyers, revealing the radiance of his lifetime of discovery.

Campbell explained how humankind's centuries and centuries of story-telling and myth-making have become part of the subconscious way that people now look at the world, their relationships with each other, and their relationships with the earth.

Sometimes myths that were once perfectly appropriate and served traditional cultures well now undermine our ability to effectively get along with each other. They put our future at risk.

For instance, many cultures created stories that had the purpose of protecting the story-teller's tribe from other tribes. The mentality was literally us against them.

Campbell used the Old Testament as one example. Moses brought the Ten Commandments from God to the Israelites which of course include the explicit "Thou shalt not kill." In later books God subsequently commands the Israelites to kill the Canaanites...us against them.

Those contradictions abound in the tribal mythologies that have been absorbed into the human consciousness. The many stories of love and compassion and sharing and participation are intended to show people how to behave within the story-teller's tribe. The other tribe—the people whose myths tell the universal truths a different way, whose habits seem strange, who may look or sound or behave differently—are to be distrusted and feared. Or so the tribal stories go. Campbell understood the reasons for those protective ways of thinking when the tribes were small and the woods were dark and the weapons were bows and arrows.

The mythology we need today, he said, is the mythology of the whole planet.

The world is very different now," President John Kennedy said in his inaugural address. "For man holds in his mortal hands the power to abolish all forms of human poverty and all forms of human life."

Tribal myths—my tribe against yours, my race against yours, my religion against yours, my nation against yours—no longer serve to protect. They are now self-destructive.

Campbell contrasted the wariness of our inherited tribal values with the common themes, the deep mystical roots, which underlie the world's great religions. To understand their universal meanings, Campbell invited us to read the myths of other religions, not our own: We tend to look at the facts of our own religion, but if you read about other religions, you might "get the message."

He told of an international meeting of meditative orders that was held in Bangkok. The Catholic monks and the Buddhist monks had no problem understanding each other. Those who have had a mystical experience understand that the ability to communicate that experience is always only approximate. The ways they convey the experience, the symbols and words they use, are their best efforts to describe the indescribable. The deep mystical experiences beneath our great religions are individually represented in the stories and symbols of each religion which inevitably diverge. General practitioners, and priests, clerics, rabbis and pastors—those who lead our religious functions day-to-day—get hung up on the differences of the symbols and the stories, and often overlook the common truths that connect them.

Our world is full of the tragic results that occur when we focus on the differences of the symbols.

As Campbell was recording *The Power of Myth*, the war in Lebanon was in full fury. He decried the futility of that conflict, a warring ground of the time that was a tragic demonstration of the divisive tribal mentalities that still hold sway today.

"There you have the three great Western religions," Campbell said, "Judaism, Christianity, and Islam—and because the three of them have three different names for the same biblical god, they can't get on together. They are stuck with their metaphor and don't realize its reference."[2]

As the Hindu scripture says: "Truth is one; the sages call it by many names."

"Each needs its own myth, all the way," Campbell said, "Love thine enemy... Don't judge... It is there in the myth. It is already there."[3]

LESSONS FROM THE GODDESS

Through history, cultures have worshipped deities with predominantly male characteristics—their God, or with predominantly female characteristics—their Goddess.

Campbell taught that reverence for the Goddess figure, the mother earth, was associated with early agricultural cultures: Women give birth as the earth gives birth to plants.

The early planting cultures of the Tigris-Euphrates river valley of ancient Mesopotamia, the Nile valley of Egypt, the Indus and later the Ganges were worlds of the Goddess. The river Ganges, for example, is the name of a Goddess, Ganga. It made a huge psychological difference in the character of the culture when the primary deity was a nurturing figure, one who cared for the earth.

Then around the fourth millennium B.C., the agricultural societies were invaded by herding people. The conquerors, whether Semite herders of sheep and goats or Indo-European herders of cattle, were formerly hunters. They came from killing cultures, and as nomadic herders they were killers, overcoming the agricultural societies as they moved. The victors brought their warrior gods, Yahweh, or the thunder-bolt-hurling Zeus. As chronicled in Deuteronomy, the Israelites were ruthless in conquering their neighbors.

The cultural heritage of the great Western religions was that love and compassion were for "my" tribe; others were to be ruthlessly conquered.

Campbell made the case that as we think about the world, as we follow whatever religious path we choose, that we include the lessons of the earlier Goddess cultural roots, a reverence for the earth, a sense of nurturing.

"The crucial question here," Campbell said, "as I see it, is simply: With what society, what social group, do you identify yourself? Is it going to be with all the people of the planet, or is it going to be with your own particular in-group? This is the question, essentially, that was in the minds of the founders of our nation when the people of the thirteen states began thinking of themselves as of one nation, yet without losing consideration for the special interests of each of the several states. Why can't something of that kind take place in the world right now?"[4]

"Some speak only of the interest of this in-group or of that, this tribal god or that," he said. "Others, and especially those that are given as revelations of the Great Goddess, mother of the universe and of all of us, teach compassion for all living beings."[5]

LESSONS FROM NATURE

The first storytelling mythmakers, Campbell taught, were primitive hunters. He was fascinated by the flowering of magnificent art that is still to be seen today in ancient caves, the mythic imagination that they reveal.

Campbell was taken by their beauty, the care that the artists took in painting animal images high on the walls of dark, dark caves by the light of flickering torches—a massive bull twenty feet long which the painter had positioned so that its shoulder haunches were a natural swelling in the rock. He asked:

> And with respect to the problem of beauty—is this beauty intended? Or is it something that is the natural expression of a beautiful spirit? Is the beauty of the bird's song intentional? In what sense is it intentional? Or is it the expression of the bird, the beauty of the bird's spirit, you might

say? I think that way very often about this art. To what degree was the intention of the artist what we would call 'aesthetic' or to what degree expressive? And to what degree is the art something that they had simply learned to do that way?

When a spider makes a beautiful web, the beauty comes out of the spider's nature. It's instinctive beauty. How much of the beauty of our own lives is about the beauty of being alive? How much of it is conscious and intentional? That is a big question.[6]

Indigenous cultures, especially Native Americans whom Campbell had studied since he was a child, addressed all of life as a "thou"—the animals, the trees, the stone and soil of the earth itself.

"You can address anything as a 'thou,' and if you do it, you can feel the change in your own psychology. The ego that sees a 'thou' is not the same ego that sees an 'it.' "[7]

Campbell was fond of quoting a passage that was thought at the time to be from a letter written by Chief Seattle in about 1852 to the President of the United States:

> The President in Washington sends word that he wishes to buy our land. But how can you buy or sell the sky? The land? The idea is strange to us. If we do not own the freshness of the air and the sparkle of the water, how can you buy them?
>
> Every part of the earth is sacred to my people. Every shining pine needle, every sandy shore, every mist in the dark woods, every meadow, every humming insect. All are holy in the memory and experience of my people.
>
> We know the sap which courses through the trees as we know the blood that courses through

our veins. We are part of the earth and it is part of us. The perfumed flowers are our sisters. The bear, the deer, the great eagle, these are our brothers. The rocky crests, the dew in the meadow, the body heat of the pony, and man all belong to the same family.

The shining water that moves in the streams and rivers is not just water, but the blood of our ancestors. If we sell you our land, you must remember that it is sacred. Each glossy reflection in the clear waters of the lakes tells of events and memories in the life of my people. The water's murmur is the voice of my father's father.

The rivers are our brothers. They quench our thirst. They carry our canoes and feed our children. So you must give the rivers the kindness that you would give any brother.

If we sell you our land, remember that the air is precious to us, that the air shares its spirit with all the life that it supports. The wind that gave our grandfather his first breath also received his last sigh. The wind also gives our children the spirit of life. So if we sell our land, you must keep it apart and sacred, as a place where man can go to taste the wind that is sweetened by the meadow flowers.

Will you teach your children what we have taught our children? That the earth is our mother? What befalls the earth befalls all the sons of the earth.

This we know: The earth does not belong to man, man belongs to the earth. All things are connected like the blood that unites us all. Man did not weave the web of life, he is merely a strand in it. Whatever he does to the web, he does to himself.

One thing we know: Our God is also your God. The earth is precious to him and to harm the earth is to heap contempt on its creator.

Your destiny is a mystery to us. What will happen when the buffalo are all slaughtered? The wild horses tamed? What will happen when the secret corners of the forest are heavy with the scent of many men and the view of the ripe hills is blotted with talking wires? Where will the thicket be? Gone! Where will the eagle be? Gone! And what is to say goodbye to the swift pony and the hunt? The end of living and the beginning of survival.

When the last red man has vanished with this wilderness, and his memory is only the shadow of a cloud moving across the prairie, will these shores and forests still be here? Will there be any of the spirit of my people left?

We love this earth as a newborn loves its mother's heartbeat. So, if we sell you our land, love it as we have loved it. Care for it, as we have cared for it. Hold in your mind the memory of the land as it is when you receive it. Preserve the land for all children, and love it, as God loves us.

As we are part of the land, you too are part of the land. This earth is precious to us. It is also precious to you.

One thing we know—there is only one God. No man, be he Red man or White man, can be apart. We are all brothers after all.

AUTHOR'S NOTES

I was fortunate to be among the millions of people whose lives were made richer because Joseph Campbell shared his lifetime of learning during his Wisdom Years.

I was reminded of the Campbell interviews with Moyers a few years ago while driving in a redwood grove in California, listening to Garrison Keillor's "Writer's Almanac" on National

Public Radio. It was Campbell's birthday, and Keillor was recounting how much Campbell's writing had influenced George Lucas as he wrote the screen plays for his Star Wars movies, stories based on the archetypical hero's journey. Keillor's report rekindled my interest in Campbell and in mythology, and my memories of The Power of Myth interviews were pleasantly renewed.

For me, there were meaningful lessons from the stories that Joseph Campbell told, and from Campbell's life:

● *He offers a second model of a way to create and contribute during the Wisdom Years.* While Frederick Olmsted had such a lasting impact continuing his work as he lead his landscape architecture firm, much of Campbell's impact came after retiring from Sarah Lawrence College. It was anything but a sedate retirement—it allowed Campbell to focus even more on his writing—but this time for Campbell was clearly something he understood to be a new phase in his life.

● *As I've learned in researching for this book, many people during their Wisdom Years come to celebrate the things that bring humans together rather than the things that separate us.* Campbell demonstrated that wonderfully, as he was especially focused on helping people reconcile science and spirituality.

● *As a Christian, I have personally found my environmental-stewardship work to be a natural reflection of my faith, a way to do my part to help protect God's creation.* I have Jewish, Muslim, and Hindu friends who make the same connection, who feel the same joy. For each of us, conserving and celebrating nature is consistent with our faith, an outcome of our faith, a deepening of our faith...something we all share.

Chapter Four

CARL JUNG

*Your vision will become clear
only when you can look into your own heart.
Who looks outside, dreams;
who looks inside, awakes.*

Per the American Heritage dictionary, the collective unconscious is: "In Jungian psychology, a part of the unconscious mind, shared by a society, a people, or all of humankind, that is the product of ancestral experience and contains such concepts as science, religion, and morality."

The theory of the collective unconscious was developed by Swiss psychologist Carl Jung, an understanding which he continued to develop and promote during his Wisdom Years.

In his book *Creativity Revealed: Discovering the Source of Inspiration*, creativity consultant and executive coach Scott Jeffrey described how the collective unconscious has been demonstrated in scientific fields:

> Charles Darwin and Alfred Russel Wallace independently postulated the theory of evolution (natural selection) within a short period of time of each other. Sir Isaac Newton and Gottfried Wilhelm Leibniz independently invented calculus in two different parts of the world and had to defend themselves throughout their lifetimes as to who actually originated the concept. Physicists

Erwin Schrodinger and Werner Heisenberg each wrote the wave equation for quantum mechanics without conferring with the other. Neurosurgeon Karl Pribram and physicist David Bohm formulated a holographic framework for the brain and the universe, respectively.[1]

Joseph Campbell, as we know, spent his life studying the ancient myths of primitive cultures. Campbell never ceased to be amazed, after decades of reading and research, by the similarities in the myths and stories of widely separated, disconnected cultures. He said these similarities resulted from Jung's "archetypes of the unconscious" shared by humankind, including isolated ancient cultures.

"All over the world and at different times of human history, these archetypes, or elementary ideas, have appeared in different costumes," Campbell said. "The differences in the costumes are the results of environment and historical conditions."[2]

In his PBS interviews with Bill Moyers, Campbell illustrated the collective unconscious at work by comparing passages from the Old Testament with the creation myths of totally separate cultures:

> MOYERS: Genesis 1: "In the beginning God created the heavens and the earth. The earth was without form and void, and the darkness was upon the face of the deep."
>
> CAMPBELL: This is from "The Song of the World," a legend of the Pima Indians of Arizona: "In the beginning there was only darkness everywhere—darkness and water...."
>
> MOYERS: Genesis 1: "So God created man in his own image, in the image of God he created him; male and female he created them. And God blessed them, and God said to them, 'Be fruitful

and multiply.' "

CAMPBELL: Now, this is from a legend of the Bassari people of West Africa: "Unumbotte made a human being. Its name was Man.... Unumbotte made a snake, named Snake....Unumbotte gave them seeds of all kinds, and said: 'Go plant these.' "

MOYERS: Genesis 2: "...And on the seventh day God finished his work which he had done...."

CAMPBELL: And now again from the Pima Indians: "I make the world and lo, the world is finished...."

MOYERS: But Genesis continues: "'Have you eaten of the tree of which I commanded you not to eat?' The man said, 'The woman whom thou gavest to be with me, she gave me fruit of the tree, and I ate.' Then the Lord God said to the woman, 'What is this that you have done?' The woman said, 'The serpent beguiled me, and I ate.' "...

CAMPBELL: ...The Bassari legend continues in the same way. "One day Snake said, 'We too should eat these fruits. Why must we go hungry?' ...Then Man and his wife took some of the fruit and ate it. Unumbotte came down from the sky and asked, 'Who ate the fruit?' They answered, 'We did.' Unumbotte asked, 'Who told you that you could eat that fruit?' They replied, 'Snake did.' "

It is very much the same story.[3]

The writer Deepak Chopra uses the metaphor of waves and the ocean to convey his interpretation of the connection between individual consciousness and the collective unconscious, what Chopra calls nonlocal reality or nonlocal intelligence:

Seen from a great distance, from the moon or a satellite, the ocean looks calm and inanimate, a large swath of blue girdling the earth. But as we get closer and closer to the ocean itself, we see that it is in constant motion, roiled by currents and tides, eddies and waves. We see these ocean patterns as distinct entities. As each wave is created, we can watch it crest, break, and race to shore. Yet it is impossible to separate the wave from the ocean. You cannot take a bucket, scoop out a wave, and bring it home. If you take a photo of a wave and come back the next day, no wave will be an exact match....

Each of us is like a wave in that ocean. We are created from it, and it makes up the very core of who we are. Just as a wave takes on a specific shape, we, too, take on intricate patterns of nonlocal reality. This vast, unending ocean of possibility is the essence of everything in the physical world. The ocean represents the nonlocal, and the wave represents the local. The two are intimately connected.

Once we define the soul as deriving from the nonlocal, or virtual, realm, then our place in the universe becomes remarkably clear: We are both local and nonlocal, an individual pattern emerging from nonlocal intelligence, which is also part of everyone and everything else.[4]

In *Creativity Revealed,* Jeffrey summed up the importance of tapping into the collective unconscious, what he calls universal consciousness, as the foundation-source of creativity: "Thoughts are not personal assets, but rather components of Universal Consciousness, accessible by all....In fact, we are not the authors of our thoughts; we're a mere channel for Divine inspiration in one form or another."[5]

JUNG'S JOURNEY TOWARD THE UNCONSCIOUS

Carl Jung was the only son of the local pastor in a small village in Switzerland. Jung said that as a child, he "played alone, daydreamed or strolled in the woods alone, and had a secret world of my own."[6] He later distinguished his outward, get-along-with-the-world personality, and his inward personality which was "close to nature and animals, to dreams, and to God."[7]

As a youngster and throughout his life, Jung was a maverick and a free thinker, trusting his own ideas and even his dreams more than the conventional wisdom of the day, or the theories of the most eminent authorities.

When Jung enrolled at Basel University in 1895, it was typical that he based his decision to study medicine and natural science on his dreams rather than his reading or the advice of others. He became a lifelong Gnostic, a person dedicated to understanding reality through personal revelation and direct experience.

Looking back as an adult, Jung realized that the idea of the collective unconscious was first hinted to him as a child when he noticed that the images and symbols in his dreams came from some place beyond his own experience.

Jung said that his ultimate choice of psychiatry as a profession came to him "in a flash of illumination."

"Here was the empirical field common to biological and spiritual facts, which I had everywhere sought and nowhere found," Jung said. "Here at last was the place where the collision of nature and spirit become a reality."[8]

Jung began to demonstrate his independence of thought early in his career. His research was dominated by the central question: What is actually going on in the minds of the mentally ill? For example, while most psychiatrists simply labeled their schizophrenic patients as "mad," Jung respectfully sought to learn what they were thinking. He came to understand that their gestures and hallucinations were full of psychological meaning.

In 1906 Jung developed a friendship with the founder of the discipline of psychoanalysis, Sigmund Freud. Freud became Jung's friend and mentor for six years.

It is a profound indication of Jung's intellectual integrity that he was willing to break with the world's pre-eminent psychiatrist and end their friendship because two of Freud's basic assumptions were just unacceptable to Jung—that sexuality exclusively drives human motivation, and that the unconscious mind is purely personal.

Jung understood sexuality as just one part of a larger "life force" which makes up the human psyche. And Jung believed that beneath everyone's individual personality is a deep and important layer that he came to call the *collective unconscious*, the psychic heritage of all humankind.

As we have seen, Jung's childhood dreams first opened his mind to this knowing. The existence of the collective unconscious was confirmed for him when he studied the delusions of schizophrenic patients, which contained images and symbols occurring in fairy tales and myths from all over the world, myths and stories unknown to his often uneducated patients.

SYNCHRONICITY

Synchronicity has been defined as "the coincidental occurrence of events and especially psychic events that seem related but are not explained by conventional mechanisms of causality."

Jung coined the term to express a concept that was inspired by a patient's case. In his book *Synchronicity*, he tells the story:

> A young woman I was treating had, at a critical moment, a dream in which she was given a golden scarab. While she was telling me this dream, I sat with my back to the closed window. Suddenly I heard a noise behind me, like a gentle tapping. I turned round and saw a flying insect knocking against the window-pane from the outside. I opened the window and caught the creature in the air as it flew in. It was the nearest analogy to a golden scarab one finds in our latitudes, a scarabaeid beetle, the common rose-chafer (*Cetonia aurata*), which contrary to its usual habits had evidently felt the urge to get into a dark room at this particular moment.[9]

In *The Spontaneous Fulfillment of Desire*, Deepak Chopra describes how synchronicity can be seen in nature:

> A single flock of birds can include hundreds of individuals, yet each bird moves in harmony with every other bird without an obvious leader. They change direction in an instant, all birds alternating their course at the exact same moment, and they do it perfectly.....
> The instantaneous communication we commonly see in flocks of birds and schools of fish comes from the spiritual level, the organizing nonlocal intelligence in the virtual domain....
> Scientist Rupert Sheldrake has conducted some fascinating studies of what seems to be the cases of nonlocal communication between dogs and their human companions...From ten minutes

to two hours before the owner arrives, the dog will sit at the front door and wait, as if anticipating the owner's return. Skeptics have said that this was simply a case of habit, that the owner comes home at a specific time each day, or that the dog can hear the car or smell the owner from miles away. But these dogs are able to predict their owners' arrival even when he or she comes home at unexpected times, or by a different car, or on foot, or even if the wind is blowing in the opposite direction, so that there is no possible way the owner's scent could reach the house.[10]

Chopra has a lot to say about putting the phenomena of synchronicity to work in our lives. He builds on the concepts that Jung articulated and invites us to constantly pay attention to the role of coincidence.

"To talk about coincidences as coded messages from the nonlocal intelligence makes life sound like a mystery novel," Chopra said. "Pay attention, watch for clues, decipher their meanings, and eventually the truth will be revealed. After all, life is the ultimate mystery."[11]

JUNG DURING HIS WISDOM YEARS

In multiple ways, Carl Jung served as a model for creating and contributing during his Wisdom Years.

His habits of mind served him well. One distinction between his approach and Freud's was that Freud's tendency was to always look backward, while Jung's was to look forward. Jung believed that personal development was a lifelong process, especially during the Wisdom Years.

Jung exemplified this personally, being a creative producer into his 86th year.

Through his Wisdom Years, when Jung was then a

famous therapist, his patients were stuck by his gentle courtesy, his humor and humility. He had personally grown immensely from the irritating, aloof man that he had been during his younger years. What distinguishes the Jungian approach from other forms of developmental psychology is the idea that people can continue to grow toward realizing their full potential through their entire lives. Jung was a terrific advertisement for his own theories.

Jung's most influential books were published during his Wisdom Years, and his intellectual curiosity continued to grow during this time as he explored psychotherapy, mythology, alchemy, synchronicity, religions, even flying saucers. Jung understood this time of life as an invaluable opportunity for personal growth.

A "creative illness," the second of his life, hit him at age 68 when he was nearly killed by a blood clot in his heart and lungs. At the hospital he experienced a near-death experience in which he saw the earth from space. He made a full recovery and focused on his writing which became his priority for the next seventeen years.

Throughout his entire life, Jung refused to become dogmatic. When he was interviewed at the age of 71 for an article in the *British Medical Journal*, he insisted that the writer make it clear that what Jung was saying was just his best thinking at this time. "I'm still open," he said, "and haven't got things fixed." Jung was constantly learning, constantly developing and refining his thinking.

"Thank God I'm Jung and not a Jungian," he said. He did not want to be tied down by any theories, even his own.

It was in the approach to therapy that Jung outlined that he has had such enduring influence, far beyond his own school. It is an influence that has been described as humane and benevolent.

"In therapy the problem is always the whole person, never the symptom alone," Jung said. "We must ask questions that challenge the whole personality."[12]

He was especially dismissive of the typical therapist's obsession with psychiatric diagnoses.

"Clinical diagnoses *are* important, since they give the doctor a certain orientation," Jung said. "But they do not help the patient. The crucial thing is the story. For it alone shows the human background and the human suffering, and only at that point can the doctor's therapy begin to operate."

Jung's patients reported that he treated them with courtesy, respect, and warmth. He was quick to display humor, and to admit that he was a fallible human being. He treated people as people, not as "patients."

"Learn your theories," he taught his students. "Then, when the patient walks in through the door, forget them." In the end, really helping a patient was all about one person respectfully being with another.

When he was 68, the CG Jung Institute was founded in Zurich with a mission of research and training. Jung set it up as a nonprofit foundation, and supported it throughout the rest of his life. The Institute continues its training role today, and serves as an international meeting place for Jungian students, researchers, and teachers.

Jung considered the noblest task of psychotherapy to serve the personal growth of the individual, an attitude reflected in his Institute, and in his life's work.

Jung's contributions during his Wisdom Years continue to serve individuals' personal growth far beyond the realm of psychotherapy. His ideas conveyed through his books and articles, his Institute, and his interviews and speeches influence and inspire to this day. He set in motion the quest to understand the collective unconscious. The quest continues.

AUTHOR'S NOTES

Here are some of my reactions to the life of Carl Jung, a few lessons learned:

● *You will note that several of the quotations above which elaborate on Jung's ideas are from other authors. Jung said, "I have such a hell of a trouble to make people see what I mean." One reviewer described Jung's writing as nearly impenetrable. Yet his was the indispensible role of the initial formulator of breakthrough ideas. It is sometimes the case that a person's creative contributions only fully reach the world second-hand or even third-hand. Those who make lasting contributions each do so in their own way, even in imperfect ways.*

● *Even though Jung had a nearly fatal illness during his Wisdom Years, he didn't let the illness define those years. He interpreted the illness as an episode in his life, something to transcend, and returned to years of healthy productivity—a lesson for us all.*

● *A rarer, but not unique, aspect of his life is that he had two "creative illnesses." In addition to nearly dying when he was 68, Jung had a psychic disturbance which afflicted him for years beginning in 1913. At times his illness was severe: He heard voices in his head, walked around holding conversations with imaginary people, played in his garden like a child, thought his house to be full of long-departed spirits. "I see dead people" is not a new concept.*

It is a mark of his strength of character that he regarded this traumatic experience as a golden opportunity for research—a brilliant psychiatrist was having a breakdown. He saw the episode as his chance for first-hand learning, a way to develop insights to help his patients. "This idea—that I was committing myself to a dangerous enterprise not for myself alone, but for the sake of my patients—helped me over several critical phases," he said. He later used ideas that he tested himself—such as deeply exploring fantasies which flashed through his mind during his episodes—as successful therapeutic techniques with his patients.

Jung completely recovered from his first "creative illness," which lasted between the ages of 38 and 43. His experience was similar to that of countless shamans and mystics, and some writers and artists. It left him an emotionally and spiritually richer person.

The lesson for each of us, no matter what our role in life, is that personal challenges, even traumas, hold the potential to be learning opportunities, perhaps of great value to ourselves and others.

● *The founding of the CG Jung Institute is yet another model of creating and contributing during the Wisdom Years—the launching of a new venture...one that continues to contribute many decades later.*

Chapter Five

WANGARI MAATHAI

When we plant trees, we plant the seeds of peace and seeds of hope. We also secure the future of our children.

"My God, my God," she said, overcome with shock and joy when the Director of the Nobel Institute called her on a shaky cell phone connection to tell her that she had been awarded the 2004 Nobel Peace Prize.

Wangari Maathai was traveling toward her day's work at the little village of Ihururu, Kenya, helping to distribute food to the local women.

The place she was traveling to when she received the Nobel call was north of Nairobi, not too distant from the village where she was born some 64 years before in a mud-walled house far from the modern conveniences of running water and electricity.

In her memoir, *Unbowed*, Wangari describes her welcome into the world:

> In anticipation of the birth, the expectant mother would fatten a lamb that slept and ate inside her home. While the women gathered the ritual foods, the child's father would sacrifice the lamb and roast a piece of the flesh. The bananas and the potatoes would also be roasted and along with the meat and the raw sugarcane given to

the new mother. She would chew small pieces of each in turn and then put some of the juice into the baby's tiny mouth. This would have been my first meal. Even before breast milk, I would have swallowed the juice of green bananas, blue-purple sugarcane, sweet potatoes, and a fattened lamb, all fruits of the local land.[1]

Maathai considered herself a child of her native soil as much as of her father and mother. She was born in the foothills of the Aberdare Mountain Range, grandly overseen by Mount Kenya from the north…an area of green and fertile farms. It was an abundant land where reliable rains supported ferns, shrubs, and trees—trees that provided fodder for livestock, and firewood, fruits, and nuts for the villagers.

Because of the regular rains and rich, dark, red-brown soils, the fields grew bountiful crops of beans, wheat, corn, and vegetables. Clean drinking water was plentiful. Hunger was virtually unknown.

In all aspects of Wangari's life, she was close to the land, attuned to nature. Her Ihithe village was adjacent to the Aberdare forest, a place of monkeys, elephants, antelopes, and leopards. Even her bed was made of wood planks with a mattress stuffed with grass and leaves.

Wangari was very close to her mother, who was the farmer of the family. Her mother planted, and taught Wangari to plant, sweet potatoes, corn, beans, millet, arrowroots, and pyrethrum, the latter a plant that served as an insecticide that was imported by the British, the only cash crop that native Kenyans were allowed to grow.

They did not have refrigerators, so each day they harvested food for that evening, typically green vegetables and root crops such as arrowroots and sweet potatoes. Her mother would bring the food she had cooked outdoors and the extended family would eat it under the star-filled night sky. Those meals were where the women and children cultivated the art of telling stories around the fire, the length of the story depending on the time needed to cook each food. The stories often pitted good against evil, with good the victor. They reflected her environment and the values of her Kikuyu people. Wangari remembered these gatherings as a place "where children were told living stories about the world around them, and where you cultivated the soil and the imagination in equal measure."[2]

When her early-planted beans produced their first flowers, Wangari was excited to see the bees and butterflies, which she later learned caused the pollination needed to produce the bean crops. As a child she loved to listen to the birds near her home, to know them from their calls, to learn their names.

An important childhood task was helping her mother gather firewood. In the process, Wangari learned the lessons of healthy microclimates and ecosystems in the form of practical spiritual lessons from her mother.

Scattered throughout the countryside near their village were hundreds of wild fig trees. There was a huge one near a spring-fed stream from which the villagers collected water. When Wangari was sent out to fetch firewood, her mother told her to be very protective of the big fig tree near the water's source, because it's "a tree of God."

By the stream the villagers planted banana plants, sugarcane, and arrowroots—tropical perennials which produce tubers like potatoes...all plants which flourish where there is plenty of water. The arrowroots were planted along the steam banks. Their big green leaves served as a hideaway for little Wangari to sit under. The leaves were big enough to cup drinking water from the stream.

In the stream underneath the arrowroot's overhanging leaves would be thousands of beautiful little frogs' eggs which Wangari would play with by the hour. After returning to the stream many times, one day the eggs would disappear and she would see the water alive with wriggling tadpoles. Soon the tadpoles would disappear and she would see frogs hopping around near the stream. In later years when she was in school, lessons on the life cycle of amphibians were very real to her.

In *Unbowed*, Wangari would write of that experience:

> In my mind's eye I can envision that stream now: the crystal-clear water washing over the pebbles and grains of soil underneath, silky and slow moving. I can see the life in that water and the shrubs, reeds, and ferns along the banks, swaying as the current of the water sidles around them. When my mother would send me to fetch water, I would get lost in this fascinating world of nature until she would call out, "What are you doing under the arrowroots? Bring the water!"
>
> I later learned that there was a connection between the fig tree's root system and the underground water reservoirs. The roots burrowed deep into the ground, breaking through the rocks beneath the surface soil and diving into the underground water table. The water traveled up along the roots until it hit a depression or weak place in the ground and gushed out as a stream. Indeed, wherever these trees stood, there were likely to be streams. The reverence the community had for the fig tree helped preserve the stream and the tadpoles that so captivated me. The trees held the soil together, reducing erosion and landslides. In

such ways, without conscious or deliberate effort, these cultural and spiritual practices contributed to the conservation of biodiversity.[3]

USING THE BLESSING OF EDUCATION

At the age of eight, Wangari began her formal schooling—anything but a given for a girl of Kenya at that time—first at the local primary school with her brothers, then at a boarding school, St. Cecilia's Intermediate Primary School at the Mathari Catholic Mission in Nyeri. There she became fluent in English and converted to Catholicism. She completed her studies at the top of her class, and was granted admission to the only Catholic high school for girls in Kenya, Loreto High School Limuru.

At that time, John F. Kennedy, then a United States Senator, funded a program through the Joseph P. Kennedy Jr. Foundation which made it possible to provide Western educations to promising students from Africa. In 1960 Maathai was one of 300 Kenyans chosen to study at American universities.

She received a scholarship to study at Mount St. Scholastica College (now Benedictine College), in Atchison, Kansas, where she majored in biology. After receiving her Bachelor of Science degree, Maathai studied at the University of Pittsburgh for a master's degree in biology, studies which were funded by the Africa-America Institute.

During her time in Pittsburgh, she experienced environmental restoration first hand as local civic leaders and environmentalists pushed to rid the city of air pollution and industrial blight along the city's now-beautiful riverfront area.

Maathai returned to Kenya and found a job as a research assistant in the School of Veterinary Medicine at the University College of Nairobi. She subsequently completed her doctorate, studying at the Universities of Giessen and Munich in Germany, then at the University College of Nairobi where she was granted a Doctorate of Anatomy—the first Eastern African woman to receive a Ph.D.

While serving as a lecturer at the University of Nairobi, Maathai became involved in various civic organizations concerned with the pressing issues of the day, groups including the Kenya Red Cross Society, Environment Liaison Centre, and the National Council of Women of Kenya. Through her volunteer work, it became clear to her that the root of so many of Kenya's pressing problems was the degradation of the environment.

ENVIRONMENTAL CHALLENGES

The forests of Kenya are precious. Much of the country is arid, semi-arid, or desert, and Kenya's forests grow only in the one third of the land that is arable. The British colonial administration had burned many indigenous forests and replaced them with plantations of exotic trees selected for the timber industry. After independence, under corrupt and incompetent Kenyan self-rule, the burning continued as lush, biologically diverse forests were replaced by coffee and tea plantations for the cash market.

As Maathai traveled the countryside for her university work she saw rivers thick with topsoil washed from commercial tree plantations that had replaced indigenous forests. Soils that had been held in place by a protective cover of trees, bushes, and grasses were being washed away from under coffee and tea plants.

In much of the country, including areas where hunger was unknown during her childhood, the crops were scanty and the people were malnourished. The cows were so skinny that she could count their ribs. By the early 1970s, clean water was becoming scarce and landslides were becoming common. The devastating effects of soil erosion caused by deforestation were everywhere to be seen.

The national dilemma was symbolized by the disappearance of the revered fig tree of her childhood, the one her mother had called "a tree of God." Someone had obtained the land where the huge tree had stood. The new owner thought the tree to be an inconvenient nuisance because it took up so much space. He cut it down to plant more tea.

It came as no surprise that after the tree was removed, the sublime stream that she had so treasured—the one shaded by arrowroot leaves and alive with tadpoles—dried up. No more banana plants or children were to be nurtured by that special place.

THE DECISION

Ralph Waldo Emerson said, "Once you make a decision, the universe conspires to make it happen." Especially when the decision is backed up by courage, passion, love, and hard work.

Many factors contributed to *the* decision of Maathai's life—her decision to dedicate her life to planting trees. One was of course the personal experiences of her childhood. She *knew* the land in all of its abundance—the trees, the soils, the crops, the birds, the wildlife. Since her first tastes as a newborn, the land was part of her, part of her soul.

She was able to combine that instinctual understanding with academic knowledge. She had studied genetics in college, for example, as well as seen as a child how a mixture of crops insured ample food during all kinds of weather and in all seasons. So when she was in a conversation at a nonprofit environmental organization about biological diversity, the discussion had special meaning and relevance.

It was fortunate that the United Nations Environment Programme (UNEP) established its headquarters in Nairobi, the only UN agency devoted to environmental issues, and the only one headquartered in the developing world. So she had the opportunity to connect with global leaders whose lives were focused on these issues.

Another reason Maathai focused on improving the environment was the work she was carrying out to improve the lives of women. Maathai was a member of the National Council of Women of Kenya (NCWK), an umbrella organization of women's groups from throughout the country. The leadership of the organization was drawn from successful professional women who had a strong moral commitment to the welfare of all of the women throughout the country, including especially the many rural poor.

One woman reported on research that she had conducted which found children in central Kenya suffering from serious malnutrition. That report was especially surprising and relevant for Maathai because that is where she came from, an area she knew to be one of the most fertile in Kenya.

In the time after Maathai's childhood, many farmers had changed to cash crops to sell on the international market, crops grown on land once used to produce nutritious foods for local families.

As a result, women were feeding their children processed foods such as white bread and corn flour, foods high in carbohydrates but low in vitamins, proteins, and minerals. An additional factor causing the change was that deforestation had reduced the supply of fuelwood, and the processed foods required less energy to cook than the foods Maathai had eaten as a child. Because of the firewood shortage, women were using materials for cooking fuel such as corn stocks and husks left from the harvest. The researcher concluded that the firewood shortage was a direct cause of the malnutrition, and the most vulnerable, the elderly and the children, were especially at risk.

Because of Maathai's direct, personal experiences as a child, she knew it just should not be that way on this fertile, well-watered land.

An additional factor guiding Maathai's path was the need for jobs. As a consequence of historic colonial policies, and later land giveaways to cronies of Kenyan political leaders, many indigenous Kenyans were forcibly removed from their traditional lands. Jobs were desperately needed throughout the country.

Some would say there is no such thing as a coincidence. It's certainly the case that Maathai was seeking solutions for Kenya's challenges at the same time that women throughout the world were recognizing the need to improve their lives and their status, and some male-dominated political organizations were giving them the space to do so. The International Women's Year was declared in 1975, and 4,000 women from around the world met in Mexico City for the first UN conference on women.

Maathai's education, and her time in the United States, had taught her not to bemoan the problem, but to think of solutions, to seek actions, to ask the simple question, "What can I do?"

That simple question opened her heart to her life's calling. She said, "It just came to me: Why not plant trees?"[4]

THE GREEN BELT MOVEMENT—SUCCESS BUILT ON "FAILURES," THE POWER OF PERSISTENCE

Author Deepak Chopra counsels his readers to set clear intentions, but not to get hung up on exactly how they will be accomplished. Instead, he advises to be alert to the "coincidences" that present themselves, and use them to chart your course, erratic though the path may seem.

Maathai's Greenbelt Movement story is one of trial and error, of routes explored and abandoned, of successes built on failures, of lessons learned, of a process of constant improvement. Her life's work is a lesson on the value of vision combined with flexibility and persistence.

Initial approaches were seldom the ultimate solution. Sometimes they simply failed:

- Maathai started a business which tried to hire poor people to quickly plant rich people's gardens. It turned out the rich just didn't want poor people around.
- Seedling trees were initially provided to the Greenbelt Movement by the government forestry agency. Depleted supplies and professional jealousy ended that idea.
- Initial large-scale tree nurseries were convenient for visitations by Greenbelt Movement staff, but mighty inconvenient for the women who tended them who had to walk miles each day. Smaller local nurseries proved better.
- Paying women only after seedling trees were sprouted was good. Paying them only after they had survived at least six months after being planted was better.

And so forth. Maathai's work was a testament to the power of persistence—trying a new way, dropping it if it didn't work, improving it if it could be improved, expanding it if successful.

Because creating jobs was such a priority for Kenya and Maathai personally, her first tree-planting attempt was to start a business which she called Envirocare Ltd. Maathai's neighborhood contained some of the richest and some of the poorest parts of Nairobi. The wealthy areas had large estates with lavish gardens. Maathai didn't think the gardens looked well-maintained, and her business would change that. The concept was for her to hire a group of unemployed people who she would train to plant and care for trees, shrubs, and flowers. When the owner was away during the day, a team of her employees would sweep in and clean, weed, plant, prune, and tend the garden. The owner would come home that evening to find the garden luxuriant and renewed, without having to have servants fussing over it day after day.

Maathai would hire people from the neighborhood, train them well, and give them urgently needed jobs. And a beautiful Nairobi would be created.

It was a perfect solution! She thought.

Unfortunately the wealthy people weren't keen on poor people hanging around their homes, even for a day or two. And the homeowners wouldn't pay in advance, and her workers couldn't afford to wait until the end of the month to be paid—the time-worn cash-flow challenge of a start-up business.

After trying to sell seedlings without success, the business failed. Maathai was convinced that planting trees was important, but she hadn't figured out how to make it work. Yet.

As a result of Maathai's friendships with the leadership of the United Nations Environment Programme (UNEP), and her work with the Environment Liaison Centre, UNEP made it possible for her to attend Habitat I, the first UN conference on human settlements, in Vancouver, Canada, for two weeks in 1976. One of the solutions that conference participants emphasized was the need to create greener cities with more vegetation, especially trees. Maathai was inspired by speakers such as Margaret Mead and

Mother Theresa, the beauty of British Columbia, and the women leaders she met from around the globe who shared her concern for the environment. Even though her business had failed, she returned home to Kenya more determined than ever to find a way to plant trees.

In 1977 the National Council of Women of Kenya (NCWK) invited her to talk about her experiences at Habitat I and subsequently elected her to its Executive Committee and its Standing Committee on Environment and Habitat. She again proposed tree planting as a way NCWK could assist its rural members and meet the women's needs.

On June 5, 1977, Kenya helped celebrate World Environment Day with a procession and tree-planting ceremony organized by NCWK. Seven trees were planted, including the nandi flame, broad-leaved cordia, African fig tree, and East African yellow wood. Those seven trees were the first "green belt."

In September 1977, the NCWK organized delegates to the UN Conference on Desertification in Nairobi to plant their second green belt on a nearby women-owned farm. Josiah Njonjo and Richard St. Barbe Baker were among the tree planters.

Shortly after the conference, they tried to establish the Green Belt Movement in numerous places in Kenya, including areas that received little rain. The trees didn't last long. Maathai learned that the local people must be committed to the project and willing to work together if the trees were to survive.

She also learned that tree planting needed to fit within the context of the local culture. A project that brought the point home was urged by a woman's group in a dry area on the traditional lands of the Maasai people. Since water would need to be hauled to keep the trees alive in the nursery, they gave the community two donkeys to carry the water. Traditionally, the

Maasai use donkeys to transport household goods, not to cart water. So using the donkeys to relieve the women of water-carrying duties didn't meet with the approval of the male leaders in the community who decided to use the donkeys elsewhere. Let the women carry the water, they said, and the trees soon died in the arid conditions.

This experience, among others, showed Maathai the need to engage the local people in designing the project around their culture and values, to make sure they're invested in its success.

News of the tree-planting initiatives spread widely and by late 1977 churches, farmers, and schools wanted to set up their own projects. This was the beginning of one leg of the Green Belt Movement's ultimate success—supporting local communities in taking ownership of the projects. The Green Belt Movement was taking root.

As opportunities and expenses increased, Maathai was constantly asking people she knew with means to sponsor trees. Institutions became interested: NCWK and Mobile Oil (Kenya) contributed some funds; the Canadian ambassador provided the use of a car.

As tree-planting became popular, NCWK received a barrage of requests for seedlings. Maathai had big plans: She wanted to plant 15 million trees, one for every person in Kenya. She asked the government's chief conservator of forests for help, and after laughing about the ambition of her goal, he said, "You can have all the seedlings you like...free of charge."[5]

When the Green Belt Movement exceeded the supply of available seedlings in just a few months, he said they'd have to begin paying for the trees. Maathai suspected there was professional jealousy at work as the women became so effective at planting trees.

Initially, seedlings were distributed through farmers and groups of women who went to the nearest forester in the area, and NCWK would reimburse the Department of Forests for the trees. There were several problems with this. Many of the forestry sites were far from where they would be planted, and there wasn't money or a way to transport the women and the trees. Also, when the trees were uprooted from the nursery they didn't have enough soil on the roots to insure their viability, which resulted in many of the trees dying before they were planted.

Importantly, the foresters were growing a small number of exotic species of trees. The values of the indigenous trees—their genetic diversity and their resilience to the diverse conditions in the countryside—were lost in the process.

This "failure" became a great success of the Green Belt Movement: Instead of using a relatively few exotic species grown by the government foresters, the women learned to propagate trees from the seed of local, indigenous trees.

The professional foresters were dismissive of the effort. "You need people with diplomas to plant trees,"[6] they said.

But Maathai knew from her life-experience that these women, though illiterate, were farmers: They knew how to make things grow.

Again, the Green Belt Movement tried things out, and evolved the process as they went. At first they gave the women seeds, but that created a dependent relationship, and the seeds were typically not local to the area. That wouldn't bring about the species diversity so important to fostering a national system of sustainable plantings. To meet the need, Maathai encouraged the women to collect and grow seeds from the fields and forests in their area. They also encouraged the women to try out different ways to propagate the seeds.

To no one's surprise, except the professional foresters, the women proved to be inventive and resourceful. They used the materials and technology at hand, and they used them well. Sometimes they planted seeds in broken pots and placed them out of the reach of their chickens and goats, which would love to eat the tasty seedlings if given a chance. The women punched holes in old cans to water their seedlings. They were encouraged to constantly try out new ways of doing things, and spread the word when a new idea worked.

The Green Belt Movement gave the tree planters an important incentive: They paid the equivalent of about four U.S. cents a tree, a real motivation for the poor women of rural Kenya.

Maathai broke the work down to a simple ten-step process—from forming a group and locating a nursery site, through follow-up after planting to ensure the trees' survival.

"By the time you get to the tenth step we'll bring you the money. You'll know you'll have done a good job,"[7] they were told.

After the women had planted trees on their own farm, they were encouraged to convince others nearby to do the same. Maathai described this as a breakthrough, because it created a self-replicating process, and a network of tree-planting communities empowering one another for their shared benefit.

The women were encouraged to plant in rows of at least a thousand trees "to form green 'belts' that would restore to the earth its cloth of green. This is how the name Green Belt Movement began to be used. Not only did the 'belts' hold the soil in place and provide shade and windbreaks, but also they re-created habitat and enhanced the beauty of the landscape."[8]

Thus the basic tenants of the Green Belt Movement were established—working with local people within the context of the local culture, and using seed sources from local, indigenous trees.

In his book *Earth in the Balance: Ecology and the Human Spirit*, Al Gore wrote of the importance of this aspect of the Green Belt Movement: "Their tree nurseries now serve as genetic storehouses of indigenous food plants carefully matched to the microenvironments of different altitudes and soil types in various areas of Kenya."[9]

It is difficult to overemphasize the visionary significance of this model. Through untold centuries of evolution, our forests have become bountiful genetic storehouses—rich with, as told in Genesis, "the fruit tree that yields fruit according to its kind, whose seed is in itself, on the earth."

As humankind has thoughtlessly deforested the planet, the diverse genetic wealth in our forest storehouse has been greatly diminished. Countless food sources for humankind and for the animal kingdom, as well as potential sources of life-saving medicines, are at risk.

The first rule of intelligent tinkering is to save all the parts, observed environmental writer Aldo Leopold.

As we everywhere "tinker" with our planet's ecosystems, saving all the parts we can is basic wisdom. Maathai showed the way as trees are planted around the world.

PERSISTING THROUGH TIMES OF CHALLENGE

While she was developing the Green Belt Movement, Maathai was a professor at the University of Nairobi and the chair of the National Council of Women of Kenya.

Then, in a short period of time, Maathai's marriage ended, as did and her position at the University. NCWK was a modest, all-volunteer organization, and her work with the Green Belt Movement had been off hours, unpaid.

She needed a job.

One day when Maathai was in the NCWK office Wilhelm Elsrud, the executive director of the Norwegian Forestry Society stopped by. Elsurd inquired about the Green Belt Movement, toured several tree nurseries, and asked how his Society might work with the Movement. A few months later Elsurd returned from Norway with funding and the suggestion that Maathai be hired as the coordinator. She took the job and never looked back. Since that fateful encounter, the Green Belt Movement became Maathai's vocation and her calling and her passion.

The first substantial funds for the Green Belt Movement came from the UN Voluntary Fund for Women in 1981—seed money to expand the work. It was a serious grant, US $122,700. The funds were administered by the UN Development Programme office in Kenya, granted to Maathai's organization as they spent it. The funding allowed several young women to also be employed, working in Nairobi and in the field to assess the success of the community-based groups, provide technical assistance, verify the number of surviving seedlings, and compensate the local women. Through the grant, Maathai's vision was transformed from an idea into the planting of millions of seedlings.

When the Norwegian Forestry Society had subsequently depleted its funds it persuaded their government's overseas aid agency to support the Green Belt Movement, which it did for several years.

Throughout the Green Belt Movement's growth, Maathai constantly sought to improve the ways they did things. For a while they encouraged the establishment of large nurseries where groups of women came together to cultivate their seedlings. That made it easier for Maathai to visit the nurseries and meet with many groups at once. She realized, however, that that didn't work well for the women, as many of them had to walk several miles from their villages each day to water their trees. And since each nursery served a large area, the seedlings would often be planted on farms far from the women's homes.

In response, Maathai encouraged groups whose members had to walk more than three miles each way to establish a small nursery in their local village instead. That made it much easier for the women to care for the trees, brought about an increased sense of participation and ownership by more communities, and benefited additional farmers who now had tree sources nearby.

Maathai also improved the incentive system for the women. Propagating seedlings wasn't the ultimate objective of the organization, creating successful plantings was. They needed to make sure that the trees grew and thrived. So she changed the process so that the women would be reimbursed *after* the seedlings had been planted, and the trees had survived for at least six months. This is the way the Green Belt Movement operates to this day.

The Green Belt Movement planted ideas as well as trees. They wanted to support their clients comprehensively in a way that significantly increased the quality of their lives.

She taught the importance of good nutrition, especially the value of growing healthy indigenous foods instead of exotic crops that didn't do well in the local soils. She urged that people have a sense of personal responsibility for matters that influenced their quality of life.

As Maathai reported in *Unbowed*, "Eventually, the Green Belt Movement would help establish more than six thousand nurseries, managed by six hundred community-based networks; involve several hundred thousand women, and many men, in its activities; and, by the early years of the twenty-first century, would have planted more than thirty million trees in Kenya alone."[10]

The work soon expanded beyond Kenya. With additional financial support from international institutions, projects were carried out in other African countries which were also facing deforestation, water shortages, desertification, and hunger. This led to the formation of the Pan-African Green Belt Network which engaged groups in Mozambique, Rwanda, Ethiopia, Uganda, Tanzania, and other countries.

NOBEL PEACE PRIZE

Maathai had known many life-changing experiences during her eventful days. Toward the top of the list would have been a call she received when she was at the threshold of her Wisdom Years. The call was from the Director of the Norwegian Nobel Institute, informing her of her selection to receive the 2004 Nobel Peace Prize.

The women Maathai was with when the call came in responded to the news politely but without much understanding. The significance of the award quickly began to sink in when the news media surrounded Maathai at their next stop. In Kenya as everywhere, such news invites a media frenzy, and within minutes Maathai was having cell phone conversations with journalists all over the world.

On that fateful day, through her tears of joy, Maathai celebrated the announcement in the best way she knew: She planted a tree.

In the company of local onlookers and journalists, a sturdy nandi flame tree seedling was planted at the edge of a green yard, proudly overseen from the north by Mt. Kenya, the source of so much inspiration for Maathai throughout her life. She later said about planting that tree there, on that day, "At that moment I felt I stood on sacred ground."[11]

In honoring Maathai, the Nobel Committee was acknowledging the powerful connection between peace and the care of natural resources.

"Peace on earth depends on our ability to secure our living environment," Professor Ole Danbolt Mjos, Chairman of the Norwegian Nobel Committee, said as he presented the Nobel Peace Prize to Maathai. "You are an outstanding role model for all women in Africa and the rest of the world."

Professor Mjos spoke of conflicts then occurring or threatening around the world:

> But where does tree-planting come in? When we analyze local conflicts, we tend to focus on their ethnic and religious aspects. But it is often the underlying ecological circumstances that bring the more readily visible factors to the flashpoint. Consider the conflict in Darfur in the Sudan. What catches the eye is that this is a conflict between Arabs and Africans, between the government, various armed militia groups, and civilians. Below this surface, however, lies the desertification that has taken place in the last few decades, especially in northern Darfur. The desert has spread southwards, forcing Arab nomads further and further south year by year, bringing them into conflict with African farmers. In the Philippines, uncontrolled deforestation has helped to provoke a rising against the authorities. In Mexico, soil erosion and deforestation have been factors in the revolt in Chiapas against the central government. In Haiti, in Amazonas, and in the Himalayas, deforestation and the resulting soil erosion have

contributed to deteriorating living conditions and caused tension between population groups and countries. In many countries deforestation, often together with other problems, leads to migration to the big cities, where the lack of infrastructure is another source of further conflict.

Africa's women have born heavy burdens. But then Africa has also brought forth strong women. One of the strongest stands before us here today.[12]

HER WISDOM YEARS

Always a natural promoter, Maathai had an unprecedented opportunity to champion tree planting on a continental and global scale during her Wisdom Years. The success of the Green Belt Movement and her stature as winner of the Nobel Peace Prize gave her an unparalleled platform.

She used her chance in many ways. For one, she became a goodwill ambassador for the Congo Basin Forest Ecosystem, an initiative to protect central Africa's massive tropical rain forest region, the world's "second lung" after the Amazon basin in South America.

Wangari Maathai's passion was given a global thrust when she inspired the United Nations Environment Programme, UNEP, to launch a campaign to plant a billion trees.

Professor Maathai was a patron of the campaign, along with Sovereign Prince Albert II of Monaco. The campaign was announced at the 2006 climate change conference in Nairobi.

The Plant for the Planet: Billion Tree Campaign challenged individuals, corporations, governments, and nonprofit organizations throughout the world to each do their part to plant trees, and to record their success on the UNEP Web site. The campaign was an element of UNEP's efforts to combat the potentially devastating effects of climate change. Planting trees—which remove carbon dioxide, the major greenhouse gas, from the atmosphere as they grow—can be an important part of the solution.

Achim Steiner, United Nations Under-Secretary-General and Executive Director of UNEP, in announcing the campaign said, "Intergovernmental talks on addressing climate change can often be difficult, protracted and sometimes frustrating, especially for those looking on, but we cannot and must not lose heart."

"The Billion Tree Campaign," Mr. Steiner added, is but an acorn, but it can also be practically and symbolically a significant expression of our common determination to make a difference in developing and developed countries alike."[13]

Mr. Steiner might well have been thinking of Ralph Waldo Emerson when Emerson said, "The creation of a thousand forests is in one acorn."

A LASTING LEGACY OF HER WISDOM YEARS

The campaign launched by Wangari Maathai during her Wisdom Years demonstrates Emerson's insight and Maathai's vision: The Billion Trees Campaign recorded more than 12 billion trees planted in more than 190 countries.

Maathai never tired of promoting tree planting and the improvement of the lives of the people of her beloved Africa. Her advocacy continued well into her Wisdom Years, including when she was battling cancer—speaking around the world, championing trees to the end. Countless newly planted trees, and restored forests—a world made greener and more abundant—are her lasting legacy.

AUTHOR'S NOTES

● *As with so many environmental advocates, Wangari's early childhood experiences were decisive. Those years in Maathai's life gave her a feel for nature, for the interconnectedness of life. In her circumstances and at that time, those were experiences that just came as a natural part of daily life, not something her parents or her teachers deliberately made possible for the purpose of her growth and enrichment. That was just the way life was. That is not the way life is for most children today, which is why it is so important that parents and grandparents, child care centers and schools, now be purposeful in making such experiences part of children's daily lives. Generally, it just won't happen any other way.*

● *Ingenious solutions seldom present themselves whole. Often enough it is the failures that lead to the successes, the lessons learned from trying, falling short, and trying again. Maathai's story dramatically highlights this truth. The things that she tried that didn't work—as well as her persistence—were central to her ultimate successes.*

● *As with so many people, it was a combination of Maathai's experiences, each adding to the other, that made it possible for her to be a creative contributor increasingly year by year. Her early years directly connected to the earth's riches, her academic instruction, her organizational experience, her trial-and-error experiences growing trees, her international connections, and her personal reputation added up more and more to the impact she was able to have. What a gift for Africa and for the world that her contributions continued for such a long period of time. Her work through her entire life, including her Wisdom Years, made the difference.*

Chapter Six

WALT AND ROY DISNEY

Now I'm a grandfather and have a good many gray hairs and what a lot of people would call common sense. But if I'm no longer young in age, I hope I stay young enough in spirit never to fear failure—young enough still to take a chance and march in the parade.

—*Walt Disney*

Walt Disney yearned to innovate. His creation, Mickey Mouse, starred in the first cartoon synchronized to music and sound, *Steamboat Willie*. Disney won an Academy Award for the first Technicolor cartoon, *Flowers and Trees*. The first full-length animated motion picture, Disney's *Snow White and the Seven Dwarfs*, won an Oscar as well. His Disneyland invented the modern theme park genre.

These accomplishments and countless more, including a total of 29 Academy Awards, did not tempt Walt to focus on past successes, to rest on his laurels.

As he approached his Wisdom Years, Walt wanted to create the city of the future. He starred in a 25 minute promotional film that described his plans for EPCOT—Experimental Prototype Community of Tomorrow. In the film Walt outlined the plans and the thinking behind them, concepts which he said would be revised over and over during the planning process.

He spoke of the innovative mind-set behind his city-of-the-future vision. What was to become Walt Disney World included a Magic Kingdom with features evocative of Disneyland in California, albeit on a larger scale—attractions such as Main Street USA and Cinderella's Castle.

But the big deal for Walt was EPCOT, which was to be a functional city where 20,000 people lived and worked. The plans themselves were revolutionary, the attitude behind them even more so.

Walt had long ago learned the emotional power behind circles—his wildly popular Mickey Mouse was mostly a collection of circles—and EPCOT was laid out as a giant circle, actually several concentric circles. The design was like a wheel with spokes. In the center would be a 30-story hotel, EPCOT's visual focal point, surrounded by the commercial core. The next outer ring would be apartment buildings, then a green belt ring with parks and recreation areas. The largest outer ring would be neighborhoods of single-family homes.

The transportation system was to be a major innovation. The compact commercial core was to be a pedestrian area: Roads for cars would be underground, and truck roads would be at a level below the cars.

A monorail would connect EPCOT's core with where people worked such as a nearby industrial park and other parts of Disney World such as the Magic Kingdom. Electric people movers—small continuously running open cars on rails—would follow the spokes of the wheel, providing convenient transportation between EPCOT's core and the homes in the outermost ring.

EPCOT was to be green and quiet, the pedestrian was to be king. Walt figured that residents would generally only need their cars on weekends for pleasure driving. EPCOT was to be connected to the Magic Kingdom via monorail so that the residents would not have to use their cars to commute to work there. The conception behind the planned industrial park was an innovation as well. Walt conceived of it as a showplace of American free enterprise. He would encourage the nation's most innovative companies to set up operation there, with an eye to demonstrating their latest and greatest to visitors. He hoped it would consist of research laboratories, computer centers, and experimental manufacturing plants for major corporations.

He saw the industrial processes and products of the future as visitor attractions. Walt wanted EPCOT to inspire the companies that operated there, and the visitors who saw them in action, to accelerate and cross-pollinate the innovations that would make the future better for all.

Walt envisioned EPCOT as a continual experiment, constantly changing, incorporating the best innovations to meet people's needs. He hoped that EPCOT would be a major influence in inspiring the future of city living.

WHEN YOU WISH UPON A STAR

Walt Disney's life was all about helping people know that their dreams can come true.

With the sometimes cantankerous but always indispensible help of his brother Roy, millions of people adopted that optimism as their own.

In 1920 Walt began his career in Kansas City making simple cartoons and advertisements with a partner named Ub Iwerks. The business failed, and Walt moved to Hollywood. Walt convinced Roy and Ub to join him, and they started another business making cartoons. Walt's creative drive, Ub's prolific drawing, and Roy's business sense resulted in a series of increasingly successful and profitable silent cartoons. Then, in 1928, they lost control of their most popular character, a rabbit named Oswald, to a distributor.

After Walt received the bad news, on the train

ride back to Los Angeles from New York, he sketched out the idea for his next character, which was brought to life by Ub Iwerks—an animated creature named Mickey Mouse.

Mickey Mouse seemed to be inspired by Charlie Chaplin's tramp: He was upbeat, optimistic, a scrappy survivor, a character with personality. Mickey achieved stardom as a result of Walt's drive for innovation when Walt synchronized the cartoons to sound, beginning with *Steamboat Willie*. In the film Mickey rescues Minnie from an evil steamboat captain. But the big deal was the sound, which Walt knew how to use in an entertaining, creative way. A famous scene has Mickey using several animals as a make-shift orchestra: The tail of a goat is cranked as a hurdy-gurdy, a cat's tail is strummed as a bass. "It growls, whines, squeaks, and makes various other sounds that add to its mirthful quality,"[1] reported the *New York Times*. Audiences were swept away, and Mickey quickly became a worldwide hit.

Walt gave Mickey and Minnie a collection of costars including Donald Duck, Pluto, and Goofy. He soon launched his *Silly Symphonies* series, with skeletons, trees, and rocks dancing to the music. Disney produced the first Technicolor cartoon, *Flowers and Trees*, which garnered the first of many Academy Awards for the studio.

In 1937, in the teeth of the Great Depression, Walt bet the company on the first ever feature-length animated motion picture, the phenomenally successful *Snow White and the Seven Dwarfs*. A series of beloved classics followed—*Pinocchio, Bambi, Fantasia*.

World War II cut off the studio's foreign profits, essential for recouping the high front-end expenses of animation, and the company stayed afloat by making military and industrial films.

Walt's gifts did not include illustration: After his

crude personal efforts in Kansas City, the animation was carried out by talented hired experts. But Walt excelled at leading, inspiring, and driving the creative process. According to author Joe Flower:

> [Walt] tinkered with the stories, told them and retold them to the animators, acted out the parts, grimacing, hooting, crawling on all fours, going over scene after scene. Similarly, he was no machinist, but he invented contraptions to make the filming of animated features more productive, or appear more realistic. One invention, for instance, was a multiplane camera: instead of photographing one inked "cel" held flat, the camera would shoot down through several planes of glass, each partially painted with elements of the foreground. As characters in the background walked through a forest or a castle, the foreground elements would shift, giving a three-dimensional impression.[2]

In the 1950s and 1960s, Walt found a big market in live-action films for family audiences—historical adventures such as *Treasure Island, The Story of Robin Hood, 20,000 Leagues under the Sea, Davey Crockett—King of the Wild Frontier*; comedies such as *Parent Trip* and *The Absent-Minded Professor*; and less expensive animal pictures, True-Life Adventures and True-Life Fantasies.

The company continued to produce animated features during this period including *Cinderella, Alice in Wonderland, Peter Pan, Lady and the Tramp*, and *Sleeping Beauty*.

Walt was the proverbial right person at the right place at the right time. It is no coincidence that the years 1946 to 1964 were the baby boom years, and the times of the greatest financial success of Disney movies. During those years growing numbers of young suburbanites were looking for family-friendly entertainment for their children. Disney caught the spirit of those times perfectly, and actually helped create that spirit, which proved to be a business windfall for the company. In the process Walt Disney became an American icon. Again, Joe Fowler:

> The Disney animated films, and the best of the live-action films, carried special value that began to emerge more clearly as the company matured. Because they were based on timeless tales that were not subject to fashion, because their production qualities were so high, because children formed a substantial part of their audiences, and because Disney had been careful to keep full control of them, the films could be released over and over, every five or seven years. And since the first release had paid off a film's expenses, almost all the money made on the rerelease was profit.[3]

In commenting on the social impact of Disney movies, Mark Pinsky summed up "The Gospel According to Disney" in his book by that name: "Good is always rewarded; evil is always punished. Faith is an essential element—faith in yourself and, even more, something *greater* than yourself, some higher power. Optimism and hard work complete the basic canon."[4]

While the movie business flourished, what stirred Walt's passions most, as it always had, was the next new thing.

In the early 1950s, the next new thing for Walt was a new kind of leisure place for families. For years he had been disappointed by the kind of carnivals and amusement parks where he took his daughters for family outings. They tended to be dirty places with bad-tasting food and bad-smelling operators. He craved a wholesome place that the entire family would enjoy. He began to think that he could create it himself.

Walt began to envision a new kind of leisure place, one with areas and attractions built around stories. The concept that began to take shape in his mind was more like a park with beautiful trees and flowers and fountains—a park peopled with Disney's most popular characters.

As was his habit with Walt's new schemes, Roy at first failed to see the merit of it: He could envision neither magic nor profit.

To move it forward, Walt spent his own money to plan the project, cashing in his life insurance. But he figured he needed at least $2 million to build it, and he cast about for a way to fund it. The answer, it turned out, came from television.

In the 1950s the Hollywood movie establishment felt seriously threatened by the new medium as TV sets were brought into American homes for the first time, by the millions.

For Walt, television became his key partner for what was to become Disneyland—in marketing the park as well as in financing it. At the time, the ABC network was trying to establish itself against much-stronger CBS and NBC. ABC needed big names and big ideas to draw viewers to its upstart enterprise.

In keeping with the pattern of his life, by this time Roy had become a convert to the Disneyland idea, and he applied his business acumen to the negotiations with ABC. He negotiated a deal that involved Disney producing a weekly anthology series for the network—specials, cartoons, television movies, and nature films. ABC, in turn, would invest $500,000 in Disneyland and provide a $4.5-million loan guarantee, for which they received 34.48% ownership in the park.

The ABC television series, initially called "Disneyland," brought the network to the front of the pack on Sunday nights, and eventually became the longest-running series on television.

"Disneyland" introduced the idea of made-for-television movies, pushed network television to a higher standard of technical quality, and in time helped to popularize color television. At the same time it was a gold mine of free advertising for the Disneyland park. The Disney organization had invented the concept of synergy long before the term itself came into popular use.

"Disneyland" was basically an hour-long commercial for the Disneyland park and the company's movies. It opened with visuals of Sleeping Beauty's Castle, and featured tours of the park, clips of Disney films, and documentaries on how they were made.

Disney's television show, Disneyland, movies, and merchandising all fit together and supported the others. A movie theme would inspire a Disneyland attraction, and the television show would have a behind-the-scenes episode on how the attraction was made. Stores around the world carried merchandise based on Disney characters, which prompted buyers to watch the television show, which highlighted new movies, and so forth—synergy in action.

Walt and the organization seemed to have their finger on the pulse of the baby-boom generation like no one else. In the 1950s they recruited Fess Parker (who professed to be allergic to horses and leather) to play Davy Crockett in a television miniseries. When the first produced show was a few minutes short, the studio had its songwriters quickly bang out a tune to fill the time. *The Ballad of Davy Crockett* rose to number one on the charts and stayed there for weeks. Little boys across America begged their parents for toy rifles, fringed jackets, and especially for coonskin caps. Re-cut into a movie, *Davy Crockett—King of the Wild Frontier* was the box-office hit of 1955. When it came to baby boomers, Disney had the Midas touch.

"All vigor is contagious," Ralph Waldo Emerson said, and the Walt Disney organization demonstrated this truth. Walt's vigor, and his insistence on the very highest quality, became ingrained in the company culture. He had the habit of making "impossible" demands on the people in his organization, and often as not they made the impossible work. Walt's enthusiasm, the vision he held out to other people, inspired them to achieve beyond their own expectations.

Joe Flower had his take on what made the man so effective:

> Walt Disney was often called a "genius" (not least by his own public relations department), but he resisted the label. He knew he was not Mozart or Einstein. Yet the label fit in the sense that genius is not about rational ability. It is about the creative power to see new patterns, to find connections that others miss. Rational analysis is weighted toward the status quo, since that's where all the known data come from. Creative synthesis is able to create new things by finding a deeper kind of unity than the available data suggest. Walt Disney had that ability.[5]

Flower opined that Walt had four abilities which made him such a force—creativity, energy, communication, and inspiration.

All his life, Walt engaged his abilities in helping people to dream. As he approached his Wisdom Years, Walt wanted people to dream of better environments for living.

EPCOT AND WALT DISNEY WORLD

The exact impetus for the development of Walt Disney World and EPCOT is uncertain. Probably it was a combination of things.

The tremendous success of Disneyland in Southern California soon had the idea of a "Disneyland East" kicking around the organization. The enormous popularity of the Disney-designed exhibitions in the 1964 New York World's Fair demonstrated that the Disney approach would be popular in the East.

Walt was adamantly opposed to just building another Disneyland. I don't repeat myself, he said, I don't do sequels. What really got Walt's juices going was the possibility of figuring out a better way of urban living, and demonstrating it to the world. Back in the 1950s, Walt had casually asked John Hench, the on-staff intellectual of the magic kingdom, "How would you like to work on the city of the future?"[6]

Walt wanted to address the social ills of the day, in his own way. For years he had complained about noise, traffic, and sprawl in cities, and he spent hours and hours reading books about city planning. He kept three at hand in his office: *Garden Cities of Tomorrow* by Sir Ebenezer Howard; and *The Heart of Our Cities* and *Out of a Fair, a City*, both by architect Victor Gruen.

In the 1960s Walt embraced the ideology of "technocratic populism" which had the goal of using the creative, productive capabilities of advanced industries for the benefit of ordinary people. He wanted EPCOT to demonstrate solutions to a range of urban issues—from pre-school education to employment to the home environment. It would have a teen center in an effort to prevent delinquency, recreational zones, areas for houses of worship. It would be noise-free and crime-free.

But first, there were details to attend to, namely determining the location and buying the land.

After the success of the Disney exhibits in the 1964 New York World's Fair, a New York location was considered, as well as one in Canada. And the Disneys were invited to be part of the renovation of St. Louis. For many reasons, especially the practicality of weather, the number of tourists, and the availability of land, the Orlando, Florida, area was selected.

Roy's representatives went to work identifying and anonymously purchasing Orlando property through third-party buyers. To accommodate all of their future plans, and to control the environment, Walt said that it was imperative that Disney purchase a large piece of land. He wanted to avoid the ticky-tacky commercial development that surrounded Disneyland in Anaheim. Walt's vision was for the guest to experience only what the company wanted them to experience when they visited Disney World.

By mid-September, 1965, 27,000 acres had been secured, more than enough to accommodate Walt's expansive vision. Despite their efforts to buy the properties anonymously, suspicions became public that the Disney organization was behind the big land purchases, and on November 15 they held a press conference in Orlando. On that same day, Roy and Walt flew over the site to see what their $5 million had purchased.

Roy saw a business opportunity disguised as menacing swamps, murky lakes, raw grasslands, and water-logged trees. Walt saw limitless land upon which to pursue his vision.

Writer Steven Watts described the nature of Roy and Walt's relationship at the studio:

> The two brothers maintained a close, if occasionally stormy, working relationship that

endured for more than four decades. The elder Disney (Roy) stood firm as a steady emotional rock while the more explosive, imaginative, and moody younger brother ebbed and flowed around him. The general pattern of their interaction established itself early in the studio's history: Walt would come up with an expansive, innovative new project; Roy would question the costs and financial implications and counsel caution; Walt would persist, arguing and charming and maneuvering for all he was worth, and finally win his brother's grudging consent; Roy then would climb on board and find the financial wherewithal for the undertaking.[7]

However on the Florida project, Walt said that his brother "was with me from the start."[8]

A vivid demonstration was Roy's bold and effective financing strategy. By selling several convertible debenture issues—bonds that can be converted to stock—and marketing a common stock issue, Walt Disney Productions was able to spend $230 million on the project while remaining debt-free. As a fawning *Forbes* article opined, "that lovely, clean balance sheet…will be Roy Disney's legacy just as the cartoon characters and the fantasy were Walt's."[9]

As Walt was in the throes of planning for EPCOT—the most enthusiastic he had been since making *Sleeping Beauty* decades before—he told a colleague that if he just had 15 more years, he could make it the city of his vision.

It was not to be. Shortly after the land was procured, Walt died of lung cancer, the result of his incessant cigarette smoking.

Along with the deep sadness of losing Walt, the responsibility of leading the company and opening Disney World fell on Roy.

Walt Disney Productions without Walt Disney was simply unimaginable to a company that prided itself on its vivid sense of imagination. There had been no succession planning. Everyone had long deluded themselves with the lovely fiction that Walt would always lead the company.

Roy assumed the reins with the sense of responsibility that had guided him his whole life, with the added motivation of bringing a living monument to his beloved brother out of the ground of the wilderness of central Florida. For their whole working lives together, Roy had run the business part of the company and left creative aspects to Walt. Roy had only once been in the building that housed the Imagineers, the creative team behind the theme parks.

An essential aspect of the Disney World development did fall within Roy's business realm—allowing the Disney company to set up its own municipality under state law. The Disney planners believed it would simply be impossible to build EPCOT within the constraints of a normal municipality. A plan was developed for the creation of the Ready Creek Improvement District, which would avoid the normal municipal review and approval process. The plan would require special Florida legislation.

A 481-page law was drafted by the Disney legal team and proposed to state lawmakers. It gave Disney rights to have its own fire and police departments, utilities, building codes, zoning, environmental control, and taxation—to operate as its own government. Nothing as comprehensive had previously been proposed in Florida, and the legislators were not inclined to give such exceptional rights to an area twice the size of the island of Manhattan just to build another theme park. The legislation stalled in committee.

Two things moved the process forward.

One was Roy's firmness. He told his representative: "Tell them if we don't get that legislation, we're not coming."[10]

The second was Walt's voice, from the grave, his last great sales pitch. Shortly before he died, a 25 minute promotional film had been created for the project which featured Walt explaining his vision for the Experimental Prototype Community of Tomorrow. The EPCOT film was shown to both the Florida Senate and House of Representatives, and the opposition vanished. The law creating Ready Creek Improvement District comfortably passed both houses.

Roy now had the land, the money, and the legal foundation needed to proceed, the outline of a vision from Walt, and a team of Imagineers experienced at turning ideas and raw materials into magical experiences.

Roy was in his seventies, with a many-faceted entertainment company to lead. As Roy looked over the black-water swamps, barren sand dunes, and scattered groves of palmettos and pines, he knew there was a herculean construction job ahead. As with Disneyland, a crash construction schedule was required to meet the announced opening day. By October 1, 1971, the Magic Kingdom was to be opened. Unlike Disneyland, it was not to be built on dry, flat ground. The water table lay just four feet below the surface, and a 16-foot base needed to be built to accommodate the underground service facilities.

To head the construction Roy relied on two military men—a general who had been with the Army Corps of Engineers, and an admiral who had built navy ships. While the task was daunting, Roy had the right spirit for the job. He wrote a friend: "In any event, we are busy as a cat on a tin roof and have a lot of work ahead of us and frankly I am having a lot of fun doing it."[11]

The bulk of the design and creative decisions were made by the Imagineers without Roy's involvement. A pivotal decision that needed to be made by Roy was the location of the Magic Kingdom, the first area to be open to the public.

The primary entry to the property would be from two highways, I-4 and 192. The company bean-counters wanted to place the Magic Kingdom at the corner of those two highways, cutting the expense of building the roads and canals to the far corner of the property. The Imagineers and the construction people had the opposite view. Dick Nunis, who eventually ran Disney World, tells the story:

> We said, Walt left us the road map, we ought to stay with it. We have forty-three square miles, and if we put (Magic Kingdom) in a corner of the property and everything else behind it, it doesn't make any sense. We ought to spend the money on the main road corridor and draining the property, because some day it would be more difficult to do.
> That's what Walt had said: "We got to prepare the land—now." He brought in experts from all over the country to study the land.
> Roy was very supportive of carrying out his brother's wishes. Without Roy it would never have happened. He told the financial people, "I want to continue with Walt's plan. So let's quit wasting time on these meetings."[12]

In his mid-seventies, Roy made the far-sighted decision for the long-term benefit of the project and the company.

Another of Roy's visionary decisions involved the construction of the Contemporary Resort Hotel. It had been intended as a showplace with the monorail running through the fourth-floor concourse of a dramatic glass A-frame building. The construction people said it would be impossible to run the monorail through the middle of the hotel. Roy was adamant. Find a way, he said, make it happen. And so they did.

Another bold move was Roy's decision to buy out U.S. Steel, Disney's partners in building the Contemporary Resort and the Polynesian Resort, and operate the hotels themselves. Disney had no experience in operating hotels, and the buy-out increased the financial strain. Roy was betting the company on the success of Disney World.

Disney World opened, as planned, on October 1, 1971. The team had selected October, the slowest month in Florida, and Friday, the slowest day of the week. They wanted to avoid the chaos of Disneyland's July opening day when hundreds of thousands of visitors overwhelmed the park, restrooms and rides had failed, and brand-new asphalt melted in the summer heat.

Avoid it they did.

Opening day attendance was only 10,000—no surprise to the Disney planners, but a shock to the media who wondered if Walt's final dream would come true. Disney stock dropped seven points in one day.

Roy was deeply worried, but the gloom soon vanished: 400,000 people came to the park during its first month, ahead of projections, and weekends drew as many as 25,000 per day.

The formal dedication took place on October 23 in classic Disney fashion: A 1,500 voice choir sang "When You Wish upon a Star," Meredith Wilson led a 1,076-piece band marching to Cinderella Castle playing "Seventy-six Trombones," and Arthur Fiedler conducted the World Symphony Orchestra with musicians from sixty countries.

Following the dedication ceremony, Roy watched a television special to celebrate the opening of Walt Disney World. For Roy, it was mission accomplished. The land had been found and purchased, the park financed and constructed, the surrounding area prepared for whatever the future would bring.

WALT'S VISION FOR EPCOT

The Imagineers carried out the spirit of Walt's dream for EPCOT as best they could.

One of Walt's primary objectives for EPCOT was to be a showcase for American industry. The Future World portion endeavors to do that, with eight corporate pavilions. The visual focal point near the entry is the 180-foot tall geodesic sphere of Spaceship Earth. Along with guest-engaging wiz-bang technologies, corporate pavilions nearby address issues including health and wellness, recycling, and oceans. Agriculture and soil conservation are featured in an earth-sheltered building. Pivoting solar collectors top the energy pavilion.

Adjacent to Future World is World Showcase, a set of country pavilions surrounding a lagoon. World Showcase has been described as a permanent World's Fair, with pavilions featuring foods, films and themed rides from many nations. Walt loved fairs, and his architect friend Victor Gruen urged that they be woven into the fabric of the city.

Guests who take the back-of-the house tours of Disney World see the fulfillment of Walt's EPCOT vision of underground service roads and state-of-the art infrastructure. There's a bustling service city under the guest city, leaving the ground level calm and quiet and pedestrian-friendly.

As a long-time resident of Los Angeles, Walt had seen the detrimental effect of a city designed for cars rather than for people, and the resulting urban sprawl, noise, and simple ugliness.

"I'm not against the automobile," Walt had said, "but I just feel that the automobile has moved into communities too much. I feel that you can design [cities] so that the automobile is here, but still put people back as pedestrians again."[13]

In EPCOT, as Walt had envisioned, the pedestrian is king.

While EPCOT did not become a city of permanent residents, Walt Disney World hotels are an echo of Walt's plans for a residential community. Families might stay for days at a time in a themed environment designed to evoke a number of possible places—a Polynesian island, a national park, an African safari. "Or a fantasy of stopping for the night in a city that looked exactly like up-to-the-minute cities ought to look—clean, fresh, brightly lit... decorated in brilliant, modern primaries set off against stark white surfaces—and hopping off a monorail in the soaring atrium of one's hotel."[14]

No cars are needed, the trees are beautiful, the grass is green.

This was the EPCOT of Walt's dreams—as best his corporate heirs could do at the time.

THE LEGACY OF CELEBRATION

A later echo of Walt's EPCOT vision was the town of Celebration which was developed on the southern portion of the Walt Disney World property in the 1990s.

The town demonstrates the principles of the New Urbanism: development on a smaller scale, increased density of residential areas; schools, stores, offices, and recreation areas within walking distance of homes; accommodation of pedestrians and public transportation; streets that invite neighborly interaction through porches and balconies; a mix of housing for various levels of income.

Except for a couple of Disney stores in the shopping area, Disney has mostly divested itself of the Celebration property. It's on its own. Celebration has public schools, a health campus run by Florida Hospital, a mixture of private businesses, and diverse building styles. Several of the public buildings were designed by well-known architects—even a little Michael Graves post office with a silo motif that reflects the area's agricultural heritage.

Along with the residents, visitors to Walt Disney World can experience a vivid New Urbanism demonstration—a town that actually looks like it was designed for people rather than cars.

THE LEGACY FOR CITY PLANNING

Pioneering urban planner and civic activist James Rouse, keynoting a conference at Harvard University on urban design in 1963, called Disneyland "the greatest piece of urban design in the United States today."[15]

It could be said that his was not the universal sentiment.

Intellectuals loved to loudly weigh in on Disney's influence on architecture, city planning, and urban design from the day Disneyland opened. Opinions were strong; critics seemed to love it or hate it. One thing for sure: It got the conversation going. The conversation continued after the development of Walt Disney World.

Walt had lived on a farm near small-town Marceline, Missouri; in urban Chicago; and in suburban Los Angeles. He had been a keen observer as his work took him to towns and cities around the country and around the world. His approach to design was simply to bring the things he liked into his parks, organize them into coherent experiences for his guests, and keep out the things he didn't like.

As did Frederick Law Olmsted, Walt cared about the total experience. He wanted the parking-lot attendants and security people to be friendly, the entry to be a "wow," the music to be right for each time of the day, the architecture scaled just so for pedestrians. Walking surfaces were to be appropriately themed, trash receptacles plentiful, cast costumes right for each area. Heaven forbid if a cast member dressed for Frontierland would wonder through Tomorrowland on her break. Everything the guest saw, heard, smelled, felt, mattered. "Story" was paramount. It was all part of the experience, part of the show.

If one pays close attention, elements in part inspired by EPCOT and other Disney parks pop up in urban scenes throughout America: pedestrian promenades, monorails, sign-control ordinances, year-round "fairs," themed hotels.

Imagineer John Hench was Walt's foremost partner in the design of Disney's parks. Hench, a true Renaissance man, "designed buildings, developed transportation systems, worked out color schemes, and created rides, all with a special feel for the Disney touch."[16] He focused on using design to convey emotional impact.

Hench's background was as an artist. An early task at Disney Studios was painting background scenes for *Fantasia*. From the beginning he was fascinated by how art communicated and carried emotion, and he brought forward that perspective as he became involved in three-dimensional architecture.

Hench was something of an intellectual in the organization. He not only created one-of-a-kind leisure environments, but he also tried to understand their larger significance, the meaning of Disney's work. His reflections "dripped with allusions to Freud and Jung, theories of communication, mythology, and architectural principles."[17] He fully understood that the "magic" of a trip to a Disney park depended on orchestrating the total guest experience. Hench said:

> The only thing we really keep in this world are experiences. We have to give up everything else. We can't keep our favorite shirt or car. Everything we have finally wears out or we have to throw it away, or it loses its usefulness or its zest. But our experiences we keep. They're not only what we are, but they're added to that great big bundle we carry around with us—the experiences of our ancestors…Walt was trying to…really give people a kind of package experience that they wouldn't be capable of having on their own.[18]

John Hench became the theorist and the communicator of the Disney design approach. He said that Walt was "extraordinarily intuitive…a genuine mystic."[19] It fell to Hench to try to break down Walt's flashes of insight into logical, step-by-step communications for their team members and for the public.

For Hench, Disney's design of Disneyland and Disney World and EPCOT had its roots in the same attitude that had long guided Disney's movies—the expression of a basic optimism about life. "Rooted in a survival ethos stretching back to the dawn of humankind, it underscored regeneration and rejected cynicism and despair."[20]

This is perhaps Disney's lasting legacy to city planning and urban design: the architecture of reassurance.

AUTHOR'S NOTES

● *I was one of the millions of baby boomer children who Walt Disney so brilliantly targeted. Walt Disney's Wonderful World of Color was a Sunday-evening staple at our home, though watched on a black-and-white TV. At Disney movies I looked wide-eyed at the fanciful worlds he created, cried when Bambi's mother and Old Yeller died, cheered when villains were vanquished. I vividly recall first seeing Walt Disney World's Magic Kingdom as I approached on the boat crossing Seven Seas Lagoon, wide-eyed again, in my 20s then.*

● *Through my adult life, I have come to admire Walt Disney on a deeper level. I love it that he was a risk-taker, literally betting the company on bold new ideas such as the Snow White and the Seven Dwarfs animated motion picture. I love it that he stayed true to his vision of creativity and hope and optimism, that he refused to bow to the conventional wisdom, that he stayed true to his inner knowing. I love it that he was always willing and eager to learn and expand and grow—through the last year of his life. In his EPCOT film, he candidly told the viewers that this is the best thinking right now, the concept will continually evolve as the newest thinking is brought into the design process. This is a reflection of his mindset as he conceptualized the original Disneyland in California. It was first envisioned—and drawn out—as a very small-scale theme park across the street from the Disney studio in Burbank. As Walt and his team studied and planned and designed, it grew into the far larger Disneyland that opened in Anaheim several years later—and that continues to evolve.*

● *For years I consciously incorporated relevant ideas from Disney properties into the Arbor Day Foundation, ideas such as formal Traditions and Service Excellence training for team members. Many books have been written about the lessons that Disney World offers to all kinds of companies and organizations. Walt and Roy's Wisdom-Years creation continues to inspire, to cause people to dream.*

● *I cannot help but be impressed by how Walt and Roy kept focused on the future during their Wisdom Years, a spirit that likely kept them healthy and active as long as they were. During his last days in the hospital, his body racked with cancer, Walt was mentally tweaking the layout for Disney World on the ceiling of his hospital room…thinking of the future until the very end.*

● *Sometimes it's useful to state the obvious: Taking care of ourselves matters, healthy habits matter, before and during our Wisdom Years. If Walt had quit smoking, he might have lived to see his EPCOT dream come true.*

Chapter Seven

MARGARET MEAD

If we are to achieve a richer culture, rich in contrasting values, we must recognize the whole gamut of human potentialities, and so weave a less arbitrary social fabric, one in which each diverse human gift will find a fitting place.

Margaret Mead led a full and exuberant life, a life that was rich with experience, a life of her own making.

The person who was to become the world's most famous anthropologist learned the essential life skill of listening—really listening—at her grandmother's knee. She was the family confident by the time she was four, listening to her loving grandmother tell family stories hour after hour as she brushed Margaret's curly blond hair.

Margaret was her own woman, from the beginning. A daughter of two stubbornly agnostic parents, Margaret sought out religion on her own, seeing to it that she was baptized before her eleventh birthday, on what she called one of the happiest days of her life.

Margaret's family didn't need religion as their moral compass. Her maternal grandfather's creed tells the story: "Do Good Because It Is Right to Do Good." Her parents didn't know what to do with a child who insisted on fasting during Lent. Her faith was important to Margaret her whole life, an indispensable component of the depth and joy of her existence.

"Prayer does not use up artificial energy, doesn't burn up any fossil fuel, doesn't pollute," Mead would say one day. "Neither does song, neither does love, neither does the dance."

Margaret was a voracious reader as a child. She read all of Dickens, George Eliot, and Jane Austin. The simple books written for children during the early 1900s such as grammar school readers and Horatio Alger stories were forbidden to her, but she read them nonetheless, to critique the shortcomings of the style.

The family moved often because of her father Edward Mead's work with the Wharton School of Commerce of the University of Pennsylvania. Occasionally the villages they lived in offered Margaret the chance to connect with the wild Pennsylvania countryside—an emotional preparation, perhaps, for the far wilder places where she would one day conduct her famous field work.

At her father's insistence, Margaret spent her first college year in 1919 at DePauw University in central Indiana. Her instinct to chart her own course was cultivated at DePauw. Her all-wrong dress, Philadelphia accent, and brilliant mind were rejected by the Iota chapter of Kappa Kappa Gamma sorority which she had expected to join. So Margaret and four other "misfits" formed a little group they called "The Minority:" a black, a Catholic, an Episcopalian, a Lutheran, and the only Jew on campus. Margaret campaigned for the first girl ever elected vice-president of the student body.

When Margaret moved to Barnard College in New York City it was a place of optimism and intellectual excitement. While plain, mature Margaret was anything but a "flapper," that was the high-spirited era of her college experience.

At Barnard, Margaret and several other bright, independent-minded young women formed a group that over the years came to be known as "Ash Can Cats." Even among that extraordinary group Margaret was exceptional for her work ethic and her quick mind. She was well-suited for Barnard's debate squad, which helped prepare her for a life-time of formal and informal debate.

In Margaret's life, as happens for so many people, a great teacher changed everything. The instructor was Ruth Fulton Benedict, and her subject was anthropology. Benedict had discovered anthropology only a short time before, and her passion for the discipline was contagious, inspiring many of her students to make a career of it, most notably Margaret Mead.

A person who knew Margaret in college said she was "a missile waiting to be directed—she was going to be *something;* it didn't so much matter what."[1] Anthropology—the science of the origins, physical and cultural development, social customs, and beliefs of man—was to be that thing.

ANTHROPOLOGY IN 1920

It's challenging for the 21st century mind to grasp Western attitudes about the world's cultures, especially so-called primitive cultures, in the early 20th century. In 1920, when Margaret Mead was in college, European colonialism, and the attitude that went with it, was not yet at an end.

The terrible consequences of the colonial mindset have been vividly related in books such as *King Leopold's Ghost: A Story of Greed, Terror, and Heroism in Colonial Africa.* In the Belgian Congo, Leopold's minions brought about the deaths of some ten million indigenous people in the territory surrounding the Congo River. Often the deaths resulted from the Europeans' greed for the region's ivory and rubber. Sometimes natives were shot just for sport.

The concept of colonialism as an accepted form of governance, mercifully, was soon to run its course. But deep-seated attitudes about unfamiliar people and cultures die hard. The attitudes that would make it possible for a tiny minority of white people to murder black people for sport were rooted in the notions of the time that human beings of unfamiliar, traditional cultures were in some fundamental way "less than" people of European origin, almost a sub-species.

Benedict's and eventually Mead's inspiration came from a slight, German-born professor named Franz Boas. In his ground-breaking 1911 work, *The Mind of Primitive Man*, Boas wrote, "There is no fundamental difference in the ways of thinking of primitive and civilized man. A close connection between race and personality has never been established. The concept of racial type as commonly used even in scientific literature is misleading and requires a logical, as well as a biological, function...The suppression of intellectual freedom rings the death knell of science."[2]

Boas made the case that anthropology could free people, especially scientists, from their prejudices and invite them "to apply standards in measuring our achievements that have a greater absolute truth than those derived from a study of our civilization alone." He believed that anthropology was a huge opportunity and a huge need which was being addressed on a miniscule scale.

Boas' call to action was relevant, it was stirring—and it was urgent. The profession of anthropology needed more recruits and practitioners, *fast*, before the world's countless diverse indigenous cultures would be changed by missionaries and technologies and Western ways—before the original cultures disappeared for all time.

As a result of Boas' and Benedict's influence Margaret become so enthusiastic about the subject that she talked it up constantly around campus, causing registration for anthropology courses to double. This was the first evidence of Margaret's life-long talent for "popularizing" anthropology.

In her writings as a student, Margaret was already absorbing the relevance of cultural context. She urged that intelligence tests be viewed with a skeptical eye, advising "extreme caution in any attempt to draw conclusions concerning the relative intelligence of different racial or nationality groups on the basis of tests, unless a careful consideration is given the factors of language, education, and social status, and a further allowance is made for an unknown amount of influence which may be logically attributed to different attitudes and different habits of thought."[3]

Her education was serving her well. It became time to put it to work.

COMING OF AGE IN SAMOA

Margaret Mead's life story is a tribute to going for it.

Mead saw her life as an adventure to be lived to the fullest. Her spirit of adventure and her courage were never more in evidence than when she decided, at the age of 25, to take off to the other side of the world, to American Samoa, to serve as a field anthropologist. The Polynesian islands met the test of the day in her new profession. They contained mostly undisturbed traditional cultures that anthropologists wanted to study soon before the cultures were forever changed under the weight of Western influences.

The territory of American Samoa was one such opportunity, and the island enjoyed the practical advantage of having a navy outpost. As a result, ships from the U.S. regularly made call. So Samoa it was.

Her mentor Franz Boas helped her formulate the

question that was to be the subject of her research: "Are the disturbances which vex our adolescents due to the nature of adolescence itself or to civilization? Under different circumstances does adolescence present a different picture?"[4]

Mead later said about the experience of getting on the train that was to take her to the ship that was to begin her voyage to Samoa, "I had all the courage of complete ignorance...I had never spent a day of my life alone."[5]

Anthropology to that time had typically involved the measurement of bones or artifacts or other things that were quantifiable. Or it involved males studying males. Boas urged a different approach for Mead—learning how individuals behave under the pressures of their culture. Boas, Benedict, and Mead suspected that culture is as important as biology in determining how people behave...but that was what Mead was there to find out one way or another. There was no established protocol for this kind of work. She would have to invent her approach on the fly.

At the time Mead looked like anything but a field scientist. In fact, at five feet two and less than a hundred pounds, she looked like an adolescent herself. Most professional (male) anthropologists were dismissive of her plan to study women and children.

The climate she found in Samoa was not welcoming: The humidity is about 80 percent; the temperatures range between 70 and 90 degrees Fahrenheit; the rain falls in buckets-full, five times per day. Mold and bacteria thrive.

Mead lived in the home of the U.S. Navy Pharmacist's Mate and his family—near the people she was studying, but sufficiently separate to allow her to be a neutral observer. She learned the Samoan language on a crash-course basis, knowing that communicating through an interpreter would be much less effective.

Useful observation meant becoming a part of the rhythms of the lives of the people in the quiet villages on the island of Ta'u. Her main objective was to subtly work her way into the days of the adolescent girls who were her subjects. Formal interviews were not the way to learn about the girls. Instead, she casually pulled information out of the conversations of groups. Mostly, they talked about sex.

She had to learn the nuances of Samoan manners: "Speaking on one's feet within the house is still an unforgivable breach of etiquette," she wrote, "and the visitor must learn to sit cross-legged for hours without murmuring."[6] No doubt this behavior required strong discipline on Mead's part: Silence did not come naturally for her. Men headed the house. Women did not speak in the presence of men at formal occasions, an admonition which did not apply to Mead as their guest. In fact, she was often expected to make speeches of gratitude.

She learned to appear to be comfortable in situations in which that was anything but the case, such as when the villagers would cut open a dead body to try to discover the cause of death. When Mead subsequently wrote of such experiences, her readers were engrossed. While she wrote in the spirit of academic inquiry, her vivid, titillating narratives established Mead's lifelong reputation for daring candor.

The book which Mead wrote about her field work was the phenomenally successful *Coming of Age in Samoa*. The book challenged the conventional wisdom that adolescence had to be, as Mead said, "the time of stress and strain which western society made it… Growing up could be freer and easier and less complicated: and also…there were prices to pay for the very lack of complication I found in Samoa—less intensity, less individuality, less involvement with life."[7]

Mead biographer Jane Howard summarized

some of the passages in the book which doubtless contributed to its mass-market popularity:

> *Coming of Age in Samoa*…would begin with a portrait of "A Day in Samoa." In the moonlight, she wrote at the end of this tantalizing chapter, men and maidens would dance and "detach themselves and wander away among the trees. Sometimes sleep did not descend upon the village until long past midnight; then at last there is only the mellow thunder of the reef and the whisper of lovers, as the village rests until dawn." She would tell of horseplay between young people, "particularly prevalent in groups of women, often taking the form of playfully snatching at the sex organs." She was satisfied that adolescence, for these girls, "represented no period of crisis or stress, but was instead an orderly development of a set of slowly maturing interests and activities. The girls' minds were perplexed by no conflicts, troubled by no philosophical queries, beset by no remote ambitions….
>
> Samoans…had produced "a scheme of personal relations in which there are no neurotic pictures, no frigidity, no impotence, except as the temporary result of severe illness, and the capacity for intercourse only once in a night is counted as senility."
>
> To Samoans, Mead would write, the concept of celibacy was "absolutely meaningless." A youth of twenty-four who married a virgin was "the laughing stock of the village over his freely repeated trepidation which revealed the fact that at twenty-four, although he had had many love affairs, he had never before won the favors of a virgin…"

"To live as a girl with many lovers as long as possible and then to marry in one's own village, near one's own relatives and to have many children, these were uniform and satisfying ambitions." Samoans had no notion of "romantic love ... inextricably bound up with ideas of monogamy, exclusiveness, jealousy and undeviating fidelity."[8]

Mead's intention was not to say that the behaviors of the Samoans were right or wrong, or better or worse than that of other societies. Rather, she intended to contribute "to our knowledge of how much human character and human capacities and human well-being of young people depend on what they learn and on the social arrangements of the society within which they are born and reared."[9]

AMERICAN MUSEUM OF NATURAL HISTORY

Margaret Mead's life was one of transitions.

As a child Margaret had lived in sixty houses as her father moved around the state to establish extension branches of the University of Pennsylvania. As an adult she traveled to dozens of countries, including numerous major field trips in the Polynesian islands between 1925 and 1975. She went through three husbands and maintained off-and-on connections with hundreds of friends.

One thing close to a constant in her life was her association with the American Museum of Natural History in New York City. Mead was hired as an assistant curator following her return from Samoa, her first eight-hours-per-day job. Due to a shortage of conventional office space she was assigned space in the tower on the sixth floor in what had been a cataloguing room. Her tower office overlooking Columbus Avenue was to be the hub of her existential relationship with the museum, and of her independent professional life, for the next 50 years.

POPULARIZING ANTHROPOLOGY

After Mead completed her manuscript for *Coming of Age in Samoa*, she gave a lot of thought to how to promote it to a wide general audience. One idea was to write articles on similar subjects for magazines such as *Cosmopolitan*.

As would many people, her publisher cautioned her to "take into account the possible attitude of your fellow-scholars whose opinions would count in connection with your further career as a scholar and scientist."[10] She listened to but generally ignored such advice, which resulted in strained relationships with her academic peers throughout her life. She was determined to bring what she had learned—and what she believed people needed to know—to the general public.

As her teacher and mentor Ruth Benedict had said of Mead, "She isn't planning to be the best anthropologist, but she is planning to be the most famous."[11]

Mead's next calling soon came to her: She wanted to study the minds of primitive children in the Admiralty Islands.

Even today there's a subtle but widespread disrespect for the intelligence, the quality of mind, of children. To consider learning how children think in traditional societies as a serious subject for a serious anthropologist was an act of vision and courage on Mead's part—qualities she had in abundance.

The question was introduced to Mead several years before by anthropologist-linguist Edward Sapir. She was also influenced by the writings of psychologist Kurt Koffka, who had said, "The only characteristics that are important in the world of primitive peoples are generally different from those that are important in our world. The difference is apparent in primitive drawings and their relation to reality."[12]

So Mead packed lots of paper for her trip.

This time Mead traveled with fellow anthropologist and then-husband Reo Fortune. While Fortune concentrated on the ancestors of the Manus people they studied, Mead got to know the children.

Again what Mead learned challenged the conventional wisdom of the time. She would write in *Growing Up in New Guinea* that it was wrong to suppose that "all children are naturally creative, inherently imaginative, that they need only be given freedom to evolve rich and charming ways of life for themselves." The children she observed were allowed to play all day long, "but, alas for the theorists, their play is like young puppies or kittens. Unaided by the rich hints for play which children of other societies take from the admired adult traditions, they have a dull, uninteresting child life, romping good-humoredly until they are tired, then lying inert and breathless until rested sufficiently to romp again."[13]

Children's play, in other words, will be a rich and meaningful contribution to learning only as the children have rich material from the adult world as an inspiration for creative play.

Throughout the time she was with the Manus people Mead had malaria. Her strength of will was tested in countless ways in her field work, but she proved to be a model of stamina and persistence.

Meanwhile, her book *Coming of Age in Samoa* was proving to be a big success, a best-seller. Just as the book *All the President's Men* inspired many young people to study journalism in the 1970s, Mead's book opened many students' minds to anthropology, and courses were suddenly packed.

While the public was reading her books, in the 1930s Mead was planning a new Hall of the Peoples of the Pacific in the American Museum of Natural History. In addition to featuring items collected during field trips (mostly by others, Mead was never a great collector) a miniature village was constructed under her supervision.

Mead's work at the Museum reflected a remarkable awareness of the details of native cultures—details that others didn't seem to notice. But she was never especially interested in amassing great collections. Mead's male colleagues at the museum treated her with detached chivalry, or simply ignored her.

Her book about her trip to the Admiralty Islands, *Growing Up in New Guinea*, was also a popular success, but it caused less of a fuss than *Coming of Age in Samoa*.

One critic pointed out how much Mead seemed to enjoy, in her second book, calling out how small the differences can be between civilized and traditional cultures. Despite its condescending tone, the remark highlights the impact that Mead was beginning to have in helping her readers appreciate the universality of humankind.

In the decade or so after her first journey to Samoa, Mead ventured out on multiple field trips to study some of the world's most remote societies. Her numerous books and articles about her field trips helped her international readership understand and appreciate the rich tapestry of possibilities of human behavior, that there wasn't a single "advanced" society model which was of course better than the wayward "primitive" societies which needed to be reformed.

The following is a small taste of the things she learned and had to say—about the remote societies and places she studied, and what her broad perspective was showing her about the American society of the day:

- "They (the "loathsome" Mundugumor) are always throwing away infants here because their fathers could not be bothered to observe the taboos associated with their survival."[14]
- (About Aimbom Lake in New Guinea, which was) "so colored with dark peat-brown vegetable matter that it looks black on the surface, and when no wind stirs it resembles black enamel. On this polished surface, in still times, the leaves of thousands of pink and white lotuses and a smaller deep-blue water lily are spread, and among the flowers, in the early morning the white osprey and the blue heron stand in great numbers, completing the decorative effect, which displays almost too studied a pattern to seem completely real."[15]
- "The course of true love runs no smoother here, where women dominate, than it does in societies dominated by men….What the women will think, what the women will say, what the women will do, lies at the back of each man's mind as he weaves his tenuous and uncertain relations with other men."[16] (About the Tchambuli in New Guinea)
- "Cultures are man-made, they are built of human materials; they are diverse but comparable structures within which human beings can attain full human stature."[17]
- "Women find themselves more and more often in a confused state between their real position in the household and the one to which they have been trained," she wrote about modern cultures. "Men who have been trained to believe that their earning power is a proof of their manhood are plunged into a double uncertainty by unemployment; and this is further

- complicated by the fact that their wives have been able to secure employment."[18]
- "We must bear in mind the possibility that the greater opportunities open in the twentieth century to women may be quite withdrawn, and that we may return to stricter regimentation of women," she wrote about the insecurity of American women in the 1950s. "....If we are to achieve a richer culture, rich in contrasting values, we must recognize the whole gamut of human potentialities, and so weave a less arbitrary social fabric, one in which each diverse human gift will find a fitting place."[19]
- "Not an ounce of free intelligence or free libido in the whole culture....(she wrote about the Bali). Anything new or strange leads to total panic[20]...Without their trances, the Balinese would lead dreary lives indeed."[21]
- "We are forced to conclude that human nature is almost unbelievably malleable, responding accurately and contrastingly to contrasting cultural conditions."[22]

At some point before 1940, before she was out of her 30s, a transition occurred in Margaret Mead's life. According to Jane Howard, "She stopped being just another ethnographer and assumed a place, which she would keep for the rest of her life, at the head of the pack—in the public eye, at least, if not always among her peers."[23]

As young as she was, she knew as much as anyone on the planet about how to make sense of traditional cultures, and she was eager to share what she knew with the public in every way she could. The pace of Mead's life increased with her renown. She seemed to diversify and add to the scope of her pursuits, rather than replace things.

In 1940 she accepted the first of her many honorary doctoral degrees, lectured on child psychology at New York University, wrote, and continued her duties at the American Museum of Natural History. That year and throughout the rest of her life she attended conferences and led committees.

As World War II raged in Europe, Africa, and Asia, Mead and her third husband, anthropologist Gregory Bateson, agreed that the widening war made it ever more important for nations to find new ways to use power.

Her natural leadership abilities were well-used leading committees and causes for many years, and they were applied with vigor to the crisis of war. Mead saw the natural tension of a trained scientist using her talents to help win a war: "The obligation of the scientist to examine his material dispassionately is combined with the obligation of the citizen to participate responsibly in his society."[24] She was eager to apply anthropological methods to finding solutions in modern societies.

It is said that when Gertrude Stein was on her deathbed and was asked, "What is the answer?" she responded "What is the question?"

Margaret Mead claimed to know some of the questions: "How can we organize a society in which war will have no place? ... What are the conditions in a culture, in its system of education, in its systems of interpersonal relationships which promote a sense of free will? ... How can we analyze the problems of man's relations to man as we have analyzed the problems of man's relationship to nature?"[25]

During the war Mead was given the opportunity to apply her skills as a social scientist to solving the world's problems when she moved to Washington, D.C. and became the executive secretary of the National Research Council's Committee on Food

Habits. In 1942 the American Museum of Natural History both promoted Mead to associate curator of ethnology and gave her a leave of absence to serve in the war effort. Her reputation was useful for both the museum and the food committee: She had become a brand name.

During the war and throughout the rest of her life, one of Mead's greatest strengths was building networks and systems. She knew who to connect with where, who got things done. Mead was said to be 25 years ahead of her time in developing a systems approach to nutrition planning.

One aspect of her makeup served her well during her war service and throughout her life: She loved to get people together from different disciplines, to learn and to share, to challenge and cross-pollinate. No subject was out of bounds for her far-reaching, fertile mind.

Between 1940 and her Wisdom Years, Mead had a fascinating personal life as well. With lots of help she raised her daughter, Mary Catherine Bateson, and she divorced her third husband. She was fascinated by dreams, and considered a night without dreams a waste. She moved an easel into her bedroom so she could instantly paint what she had dreamed.

As she moved toward her Wisdom Years like a one-woman freight train, she used her voice in every way she could to advocate for her profession, her vision of American society, and for causes she cared about. She chaired conferences, wrote books and magazine columns, and gave innumerable speeches. She became a television celebrity: No major societal issue or controversy was considered properly addressed until Margaret Mead had commented on it.

"You're coming of age!" she reminded her United Nations colleague Mildred Leet. "People respect age! Learn to raise your voice! People will listen!"[26]

HER WISDOM YEARS

If you associate enough with older people who do enjoy their lives, who are not stored away in any golden ghettos, you will gain a sense of continuity and of the possibility for a full life.

Winston Churchill had his cigar, Douglas McArthur had his corn cob pipe, Superman had his cape...and Margaret Mead had her stick.

In her 60th year, while attending a dinner to celebrate a child's birthday party, Mead fell on a slippery grease spot in the kitchen and broke her ankle, again.

As an aid to getting around on her cast and her gimpy ankle, she sought an alternative to a traditional cane. Canes were for "old ladies," she thought, not for her.

She found her solution in a "thumb stick" made of British cherry wood. The strong walking stick was about as tall as her shoulder and was branched into the shape of a Y at the top. The cudgel turned out to be a brilliant PR device—the iconic symbol of an iconic woman—with practical value as well. Mead could use it to hail taxis, lead her way to a subway seat, nudge things off high shelves, or serve as a temporary coat rack. The cudgel was to be her constant companion for the rest of her vigorous life.

During her Wisdom Years, Mead took full advantage of her eminence, her deep and wide experience, and her broad circle of well-connected friends to champion causes she cared about.

"Never doubt that a group of small, concerned citizens can change the world," she said. "Indeed, it is the only thing that ever has."

She took her own words seriously, and was determined to use her Wisdom Years to "change the world" for the better in every way she could.

Beginning in her 66th year, she was invited by an Episcopal clergyman to serve as a consultant to his Subcommittee for the Revision of the Book of Common Prayer. Since Mead had studied rites of passage throughout her life she was asked to help with the section about baptism and confirmation. In her six years of service on the committee she was more than willing to take exception to interpretations and judgments of the official church theologians. She understood the importance of ritual to every human society, and she made the strong case that it was more important than ever in the midst of rapidly changing modern society.

She strongly made the case that people need to feel an individual connection with the timeless and the universal. Mead spoke not for anthropology, but for the individual church members who would use the Book of Common Prayer. She knew how meaningful it could be in people's daily lives.

Mead strongly felt the divine in her life, and she wanted to support that opportunity in others in every way she could.

An incident at a conference of clergymen illuminates the passion and depth of knowledge and experience that she brought to issues relating to her faith. At the conference… "a rather flippant young clergyman took issue with something Mead said about the difference between marriages and weddings. The sacrament of marriage, Mead had said, could exist between people regardless of their history or background, but a wedding, with all its pagan ritual of flowers and bowers and the giving away of the bride, was a one-time event. The flippant young clergyman said, 'Well, *Miss* Mead, what would *you* know.'

" … Margaret up and traced the entire history of matrimony, developing the theme conically, theologically, and spiritually, for thirty-five minutes. …Finally she stopped to ask, 'Will *that* satisfy you, young man?' There was great applause. Margaret was ruthless when confronted, but she loved it."[27]

Her companion said, "This gave me great respect for her not only as a friend, whom I had already come to love, but as a church person."

The work on the *Common Book of Prayer* was just one small part of Mead's Wisdom Years.

"Margaret Mead," Jane Howard wrote, "who had hungered all her life for acclaim, companionship, and a full schedule, got all three, in the last dozen years of her life, to a measure that even she must have found a little befuddling."[28]

She never stopped learning. If Mead was to become an effective spokesperson, for example, she had to learn to become effective on television—and so she did. She taught herself to establish rapport with the unseen millions behind the TV camera, one on one.

Her personal habit of constant learning continued unabated. She learned "all the time, through her pores," a friend said. "She had a brilliant flair for seizing ideas from children, colleagues, historians, and every other source that came her way. She was the greatest picker of brains I've ever known."[29]

Mead's concerns became planetary; world-wide issues, the very health of the earth, became her concern. She became a citizen-philosopher, a spokesperson for humankind.

One career-long contradiction continued: Even though she was America's best-known, most-celebrated scientist, the National Academy of Sciences did not elect her to membership until she was 74. Her colleagues in the scientific establishment never quite cottoned to her cut-to-the-chase approach.

She never lost her zest for promoting her chosen profession.

At the age of 73, Mead began her three-year term as president of the American Association for the Advancement of Science, AAAS, her most prestigious platform for her passion.

"She wanted momentum to gather for what she called the human sciences," said William Carey, whom Mead helped to persuade to take over the AAAS. "She felt that the AAAS had great potential for popularizing science, not just in the show business sense. She sensed that the arrogance of Western civilization was blinding us to the incendiary changes developing in the rest of the world, and the AAAS should accept its mandate to offset that arrogance."[30]

She took on the "hierarchy of snobbery" within the scientific world, especially the way the hard sciences, physicists especially, denigrated the social sciences.

Mead was more than willing to risk the ridicule of her hard-science colleagues by being open-minded on subjects varying from parapsychology to unidentified flying objects. She had her own mind and she spoke it.

At the age of 75 she focused on saving the planet, and she felt there was no time to lose.

For years she had annually taken week-long cruises with diverse leading thinkers such as Barbara Ward, Arnold Toynbee, and Buckminster Fuller. They hashed out the great issues facing the world, and she was not hesitant to share their conclusions with anyone, including the President of the United States. She wanted to more fully use the know-how of the scientific community, especially the human sciences, in solving the world's urgent problems.

She was an unfailing champion of the United Nations, because she felt that the UN, for all its shortcomings, was the best advocate for the cultures in the developing world. Vocal support for the UN was part and parcel of what her professional training and her generous heart told her about the importance of connectedness.

In what could have been a summing up of her life, Margaret Mead had once said it would be her grand hope for humankind to build, "from a hundred cultures, one culture which does what no culture has ever done before—gives a place to every human gift."[31]

AUTHOR'S NOTES

● I confess I cringed each time I wrote the word "primitive" in this chapter to describe the people who Mead studied and grew to know and to respect. The word is a Western pejorative, one of countless ways that have been found to cause people not of European origin, or less technologically developed, to be thought of as "less than." As Joseph Campbell and others have taught us, traditional or indigenous or primitive people are sometimes far "ahead" of more "developed" societies in many ways—in their knowledge of and respect for nature, in their spirituality, in their happiness, in their ability to live together in peace. Primitive was the word used by Margaret Mead and the anthropologists of her day. I used the word to communicate their ideas as best I could to the reader. Please accept my apologies for the disrespect it suggests. Disrespect is anything but my intention.

● In an age of ever-increasing professional specialization, Mead's far-reaching mind and her wide circle of friends vividly demonstrate the richness that can be part of our lives if we remain curious and open to the expertise and experience of others. This is a lesson for us all, not just one such as Mead who aspires to be a "citizen-philosopher." Our lives are made richer by letting in the passions and the experiences and the ideas and the values of others, including especially those quite different than ourselves.

● In her Wisdom Years Mead wanted to use her fame and her voice to champion causes she cared about, and she

made many speeches and public appearances. No doubt her speeches conveyed a lot of knowledge and insights, stories of lessons learned. But the curiosity and personal caring that she conveyed may have been even more important.

A colleague of mine recently told me that in 1969, as a student at the University of Wisconsin, he had the privilege of serving as Mead's personal host and escort throughout the day when she visited the campus to speak. He said it was a challenge keeping up with the 68-year-old, thumb stick and all, who wanted to walk by the lake near the campus, and see as much as she could. What struck him most was how sincerely interested she was in the students she met. She didn't just ask, "How are you?" She really wanted to know—what they were thinking about and learning, about their interests and concerns and passions.

This is perhaps the greatest gift that anyone in their Wisdom Years can give a younger person—more valuable than any financial gift, any knowledge or insight—the gift of caring.

Chapter Eight

JOHN ADAMS

We have it in our power to begin the world anew.
—Thomas Paine

The Boston Massacre helped inflame American public opinion, and sent the colonies firmly on the road to revolution. It was also a milestone in establishing the leadership credentials of young John Adams, but not in the way one might expect.

Public opinion in the American colonies had begun to turn against British governance with the Stamp Act of 1765. The British Parliament had passed a series of direct taxes on the American colonies to pay England's expenses from the French and Indian Wars, which ended in 1763. Americans were outraged by the taxes, which had been levied without consulting the American legislatures. "Taxation without representation" became the cry, as Americans felt they had been denied their basic rights as Englishmen.

John Adams rose to prominence as a strong opponent of the Stamp Act, which was a visible symbol, a daily reminder, of the heavy hand of British rule.

Boston was the center of discontent in the colonies, and British troops were stationed in the city to keep order amidst public anger. Of course their presence only aggravated the colonists' dissatisfaction, which came to a head on March 5, 1770.

On that cold winter evening, with deep snow covering the streets, a lone British sentry posted in front of the Custom House was taunted by a small group of men and boys. A church bell began to toll nearby, the alarm for fire, and crowds came pouring into the streets. Many men from the nearby waterfront were brandishing clubs. As a throng of hundreds converged at the Custom House, the guard was reinforced by eight British soldiers with muskets and bayonets, led by a captain with sword drawn. The mob threw chunks of ice, snowballs, and stones at the hated redcoats, and the British suddenly opened fire, killing five Bostonians.

Samuel Adams, John's firebrand cousin, quickly labeled the killings a "bloody butchery." Paul Revere published a print interpreting the scene as a deliberate slaughter of the innocent, and the incident would become the "Boston Massacre" in the public mind, a terrible expression of British tyranny.

Thirty-four-year-old John Adams—stalwart opponent of British rule and soon-to-be voice of the revolution—was asked to defend the soldiers and their captain when they came to trial. No one else would take the case, he was told.

Adams immediately accepted the case. He was a man of principle, and he was of the strong belief that no man in a free country should be denied a fair trial. As was the case throughout his long and remarkable life, his duty was clear, and John Adams did his duty.

The state of emotion was high in Boston, and Adams feared for the safety of his family, as well as the success of his law practice. He would be making a defense that ran contrary to the popular outrage. Public criticism, personal criticism, was substantial, something that Adams always found painful.

"The only way to compose myself and collect my thoughts," he wrote in his diary, "is to set down at my table, place my diary before me, and take my pen into my hand. This apparatus takes off my attention from other objects. Pen, ink, and a paper and a sitting posture are great helps to attention and thinking."[1]

He bucked himself up by copying the following passage from an eminent opponent of capital punishment:

> If, by supporting the rights of mankind, and of invincible truth, I shall contribute to save from the agonies of death one unfortunate victim of tyranny, or of ignorance, equally fatal, his blessings and years of transport will be sufficient consolation to me for the contempt of all mankind.[2]

The trials, one for the British captain, and one for the soldiers, were delayed until October to allow tempers to cool. The trials were conspicuously fair.

Whether the captain had given the order to fire could never be proven, and he was found not guilty. Adams' statement for the defense was considered to be a "virtuoso performance." His closing to the jury for the soldiers' trial lasted two days.

"Facts are stubborn things," Adams said, "and whatever may be our wishes, our inclinations, or the dictums of our passions, they cannot alter the state of facts and evidence."[3]

The facts had convinced him of the soldiers' innocence. The tragedy resulted from the actions of the mob, and the mob's actions resulted from the misguided policy of quartering troops in a city to try to keep the peace.

"Soldiers quartered in a populous town will always occasion two mobs where they prevent one. They are wretched conservators of the peace,"[4] Adams rightly said.

Adams described how the "rabble" clubbed a soldier, threw stones and ice, and shouted "Kill them!

Kill them!" Self-defense, he reminded the jury, was a basic law of human nature.

The jury acquitted six of the soldiers and found two guilty of manslaughter, for which they were merely branded on their thumbs. While there were some angry reactions to the results of the trials, there were no riots. Adams was criticized in the *Boston Gazette*, and later said that he lost half of his legal business.

But over time, his role in defending the soldiers enhanced Adams' reputation for integrity, causing the public, and leading patriots, to respect him all the more. Here was a person who would do the right thing, and take the long view, despite the whipped-up public passions of the moment.

There had been no obvious indicator that John Adams was destined for a lifetime of national leadership, of a central role in "beginning the world anew." Adams' father was a summer farmer and a winter shoemaker. His father spent his whole life in Braintree, Massachusetts; no Adams had taken part in public life beyond their little home town. Until the revolutionary days of 1774, John Adams had never been beyond New England. He had been born in a farmer's cottage, and as an adult lived in a nearly duplicate one adjacent to it.

ATLAS OF INDEPENDENCE, CO-CREATOR OF AMERICA

John Adams' selection as a representative to the Continental Congress was pivotal for his life, pivotal for America.

Adams nominated George Washington to lead the Continental Army and Thomas Jefferson to draft the Declaration of Independence, serving on the drafting committee himself with Jefferson and Benjamin Franklin. He was the central figure in the Congress, and was unanimously selected to head the Board of War and Ordinance, making him a one-man Department of Defense, responsible for equipping the army and building a navy from scratch.

He was selected to join Benjamin Franklin in Paris with the responsibility of creating a vital wartime alliance with France. His crossing with his 10-year old son John Quincy was the first of several dangerous trips across the stormy Atlantic. Adams arrived in Paris, found the alliance treaty basically completed, and returned home. Back in Massachusetts he was given the job of drafting the state's constitution. The Massachusetts constitution included provisions such as the separation of powers between the executive, judicial, and legislative branches, and became a model for other state constitutions and ultimately the United States constitution.

Shortly Congress sent Adams back to France to help negotiate the treaty to end the war with England. The treaties that were ultimately signed, called the Peace of Paris, were a successful result of Franklin's diplomacy and Adams' tenacity. Jefferson followed Franklin as Adams' diplomatic partner in France, and their lifelong bond was sealed. Adams subsequently became America's Ambassador to England, and also negotiated a vital loan with the Dutch to make it possible for the new American government to consolidate its European debts and begin on a reasonable financial footing.

The United States Constitution was drafted and ratified while Adams served in Europe, and he returned to America in 1789 to be elected as the country's first Vice President as George Washington was elected President.

ABIGAIL

John Adams made many visionary decisions throughout his long and fruitful career, but his greatest decision was one of the heart—to court and marry Abigail Smith, a daughter of a Congregational minister.

Abigail's love and wisdom supported Adams throughout his career, as did her capable management of the Adams farm when he was so often away.

Abigail was also an early champion of independence, and encouraged John in all his actions in building the new nation. Since they were separated many times—when she was in Quincy while he was serving in Paris or London, or in Philadelphia, New York, or Washington—their relationship and their love was manifest via their letters. Those letters, hundreds of them, document this remarkable partnership and provide a unique window on America's early days—both the dark days of danger, and the glorious days of triumph.

Abigail was bright and curious, an avid reader, but like most women of her time, she was educated exclusively at home. As John and his colleagues were convening to draft the Declaration of Independence, she famously asked him in a letter to "remember the ladies and be more generous and favourable to them than your ancestors." She was a lifelong advocate for the education of women and against slavery.

Adams was immeasurably blessed to have such a strong and brilliant woman as his life-long partner.

TOWARD HIS WISDOM YEARS

At the end of Washington's second term, John Adams was elected as the second President of the United States, and Thomas Jefferson was elected as his Vice President.

England and France were at war throughout his presidential term. Alexander Hamilton, a member of the president's cabinet, and much of their Federalist Party, favored England; Vice President Thomas Jefferson and the Democratic-Republican Party favored France.

Adams fervently wished to follow the policy set by George Washington when he was president, of staying out of European wars. Most Americans were pro-French as a result of France's assistance during the Revolutionary War—despite the French seizing American merchant ships that were trading with the British.

Sentiment shifted against France virtually overnight when Americans became aware of what became known as the XYZ Affair, in which the French demanded huge bribes before any discussions could begin to resolve the countries' differences. The public called for full-scale war against France.

Having served as a diplomat in France and spent years in Europe, Adams knew that America would not be able to win such a conflict. At the time France had a massive war-making capacity, and in fact was successfully fighting across much of Europe. Adams understood that despite the public clamor for war, such a hopeless conflict could not be won, and would quite possible doom the young nation in its infancy.

Instead, Adams championed a strong defensive navy and harassed the French ships which threatened American merchant vessels. This undeclared Quasi-War, which produced a number of victories for the American navy, resulted in high popularity for President Adams.

Nonetheless, Adams knew that a devastating real war remained a constant possibility, and despite the threat to his popularity, he sought peace.

On February 18, 1799, after consulting with

no-one, not even with his trusted Abigail who was in Quincy, Adams took the bravest, most decisive action of his presidency. He sent a message to the Senate nominating a peace envoy to France to seek to honorably settle the conflict.

All sides of the American debate were taken aback: Depending on their allegiances they were astounded, disgusted, or enraged. Adams' own Secretary of State wrote in one letter that the "*honor* of the country is prostrated in the dust—God grant that its safety may not be in jeopardy," and in another, "every real patriot ... was thunderstruck."[5]

Despite their angst, the anti-French Federalists did not move to strike down Adams' motion. In a compromise with the Senate, Adams agreed to a three-person peace commission. He nominated William Vans Murray, Patrick Henry, and Chief Justice Oliver Ellsworth; the Senate confirmed the appointments and promptly adjourned. After the government received assurances from France that the envoys would be dealt with honestly, the commissioners were sent on their way.

Critics said that Adams would never have made the move for peace if Abigail had been in town to consult with, but they were wrong. Upon hearing the news she called his decision a "master stroke."

Later in the year, in his State of the Union Message to a joint session of Congress, Adams continued to cool the nation's ardor for a war that he knew would be devastating. Rather than beat the drums of war, President Adams emphasized a "pacific and humane" approach to international affairs. He said that while "measures adopted to secure our country against foreign attacks" must not be resisted, defense measures should be "commensurate with our resources and the situation of our country." Instead of beating the drums of war, he spoke of "prospects of abundance," and "the return of health, industry, and trade."⁶

It was a speech of moderation and peace. Abigail said, "It has been received here with more applause and approbation than any speech which the President has ever delivered."⁷

In late 1800, Adams moved, ahead of Abigail, to Washington City, then a raw town being wrestled out of a virgin wilderness. The immense President's House was unfinished, reeking of wet plaster and wet paint. The sparse furniture brought from Philadelphia seemed to cower in the corners of the huge rooms. The house was surrounded by a rubble-strewn, wagon-rutted, tree-stump-riddled field. This was to become America's magnificent White House.

Upon his arrival Adams took out a plain sheet of paper which he headed President's House, Washington City. He wrote Abigail his first letter, offering a simple benediction: "I pray heaven to bestow the best of blessings on this house and all that shall hereafter inhabit it. May none but honest and wise men ever rule under this roof."⁸ His lines are now inscribed in the mantelpiece of the State Dining Room at the White House.

A few days later, Adams finally received news from France. The mission which he had courageously launched had succeeded. A treaty with France, the Convention of Mortefontaine, had been signed on October 3, 1800. At a celebration for the signing, Napoleon Bonaparte stated that the differences between the United States and France had been only a family quarrel. Toasts were made to perpetual peace.

The Quasi-War was over, an immense victory for Adams. He was rightly proud of having kept the nation out of war, and later in life he once suggested his tombstone might read "Here lies John Adams, who took upon himself the responsibility of Peace with France in the year 1800."⁹

The news arrived too late to effect the election. In what had been an acrimonious campaign between Federalist followers of Adams, and Democratic-Republican followers of his Vice President and once friend Thomas Jefferson, Adams was narrowly defeated. In fact, with a change of only 250 votes in New York City, Adams would have won the electoral count, and the election. It was not to be.

Adams was defeated, the first sitting American President to be turned away by the voters. This was not how Adams wished to begin his Wisdom Years.

BACK TO QUINCY

As his Wisdom Years began in earnest, Adams' life would be profoundly and forever changed. As a leading advocate of the cause of American liberty, Adams had once braved fearsome Atlantic storms in small wooden sailing ships to represent his nation in France, in England, and in Holland. He had spent months and years away from his beloved Abigail, doing his duty. He had been the voice of the revolution, an early and steadfast champion of independence, putting his life on the line along with his peers. He had helped create a nation, helped make a reality of the ideal of democracy. He had proudly led the nation as its President.

Now it was back to little Quincy. For the rest of his long life, his physical world was to be his farm, and trips within about 15 miles.

His attitude as he left the power of Washington for the tranquility of Quincy was one of equanimity.

As he left the capital, he was leaving President Jefferson a nation "with its coffers full," he wrote, and with "fair prospects of peace with all the world smiling in its face, its commerce flourishing, its navy glorious, its agriculture uncommonly productive and lucrative."

In a letter to his successor, Adams said he saw "nothing to obscure your prospect of a quiet and prosperous administration, which I heartily wish you."

Jefferson did not respond. Adams' letter would be the last between them for eleven years.

Adams was not indifferent to the personal impact of a sudden, night-and-day change of lifestyle.

"The only question remaining with me is what shall I do with myself," Adams wrote a friend. "Something I must do, or ennui will rain upon me in buckets."[11]

After "a life of journeys and distant voyages," he wrote to another friend, stillness "may shake my old frame. Rapid motion ought not be succeeded by sudden rest."[12]

While complaining was not John and Abigail's style, their first winter back home was a hard one, and not just because of the New England cold. The humiliating public rejection, the recent death of their son Charles, and their winter seclusion took a heavy toll. They felt that they were despised, or worse yet, irrelevant.

But then as now, spring has a way of reviving the spirit.

In letters to family members, Abigail commented on the restorative power of warmer days, resumed routines, and springtime flowers:

"I have commenced my operation of dairy woman, and she might see me at five o'clock in the morning skimming my milk."

She described how her beautiful garden, "from the window at which I write…the full bloom of the pear, the apple, the plum and peach," helped again fill her heart with joy. "Envy nips not their buds, calumny destroys not their fruits, nor does ingratitude tarnish their colors."

And, "Your father appears to enjoy tranquility and a freedom of care which he has never before experienced. His books and farm occupy his attention."[13]

Where the entire nation had recently been his responsibility, his domain now consisted of his three farms—600 acres of salt marsh, woodlands, and producing fields.

He was proud of his success, together with his summertime hired hands, of bringing in the biggest hay crop ever—thirty tons from acreage that had once produced only six.

Adams loved joining in the work—for the exercise, for the companionship of men he had known for years, for the pride of doing things right, for the simple enjoyment of being outdoors.

His books were another joy. He liked to read for hours every day.

In one year, Adams would read Shakespeare twice through. He read old favorites in Latin and French, English poetry and history, journals such as the *Edinburgh Review*, about every newspaper he could get his hands on, and novels by the young James Fenimore Cooper. He was devoted to the Bible, and to Cicero. Through the years had had read Cicero's essay on growing old gracefully, *De Senectute*, so many times that he nearly knew it by heart. From Quincy he quoted from it in a letter:

> For as I like a young man in whom there is something of the old, so I like an old man in whom there is something of the young; and he who follows this maxim, in body will possibly be an old man but he will never be an old man in mind.[14]

Exercise was a regular routine, and not just working on the farm. He took rambling horseback rides throughout his farms, along the ocean, to nearby farms and towns. He would walk for miles, day after day.

At Quincy, during his Wisdom Years, Adams seemed to most exercise his mind, and his spirit. His sense of wonder was more acute than ever:

> I find my imagination, in spite of all my exertions, roaming in the Milky Way, among the nebulae, those mighty orbs, and stupendous orbits of suns, planets, satellites, and comets, which compose the incomprehensive universe; and if I do not sink into nothing in my own estimation, I feel an irresistible impulse to fall on my knees, in adoration of the power that moves, the wisdom that directs, and the benevolence that sanctifies this wonderful whole.[15]

The marvels of nature even right outside his window filled him with delight, despite the damage done to his orchard:

> A rain had fallen from some warmer region in the skies when the cold here below was intense to an extreme. Every drop was frozen wherever it fell in the trees, and clung to the limbs and sprigs as if it had been fastened by hooks of steel. The earth was never more universally covered with snow, and the rain had frozen upon a crust on the surface which shone with the brightness of burnished silver. The icicles on every sprig glowed in all the luster of diamonds. Every tree was a chandelier of cut glass. I have seen a Queen of France with eighteen millions of livres of diamonds upon her person and I declare that all the charms of

her face and figure added to all the glitter of her jewels did not make an impression on me equal to that presented by every shrub. The whole world was glittering with precious stones.[16]

Before they left Washington, Abigail had written that the most distressing aspect of leaving public life would be that their ability to "do good" would be "so greatly curtailed."[17]

John and Abigail responded as they could to opportunities to do good that presented themselves.

When he was 85 John was chosen as a delegate to a state convention that was convened to revise the Massachusetts constitution that Adams had drafted some 40 years before. He was pleased that the town of Quincy had elected him unanimously as their representative.

Adams received a standing ovation upon his arrival at the convention. During the debates, he offered an amendment guaranteeing religious freedom in the commonwealth. His speech in support of the amendment was full of passion and conviction, but was insufficient to overcome the prejudice of the large Christian majority toward Jews. The amendment failed. Nonetheless the cause of embracing a diverse population in the young American nation was given strong voice by a respected Founder in an important public forum. A step was made away from bigotry.

An avid newspaper reader, Adams made every effort to keep himself well-informed on world events. He had a special pipeline via his correspondence with his son John Quincy Adams.

John Quincy was elected to the United States Senate from Massachusetts in 1803. That same year, Bonaparte suddenly offered to sell the huge unexplored Louisiana Territory to the United States—a move not likely to have happened if Adams had not found the path to peace with France during his presidency. President Jefferson, who traditionally sought a smaller role for the federal government, seized the opportunity to double the size of the nation. Jefferson agreed to the purchase, which required Senate approval. John Quincy crossed party lines to vote in favor of the acquisition, against the wishes of partisan Federalists, and with his father's strong approval. Jefferson, John Quincy, and John Adams all chose to ignore party politics and prior dogma. They took the larger view—much to the benefit of the nation, and future generations.

Staying abreast of his eldest son's activities kept him abreast of the world.

John Quincy was appointed minister to Russia, and was off to St. Petersburg. In 1814, he found that he had been appointed a peace envoy to negotiate an end to the War of 1812 with Great Britain. It was history repeating itself, giving him the same role his father had in Paris in 1782. The peace treaty which he helped negotiate was met with approval by both nations grown tired of war. He was appointed as Minister to England, and subsequently Secretary of State. Thanks to John Quincy's diplomacy, in 1819 Spanish Florida was added to the United States. His father called it a blessing "beyond all calculation."

John Adams had much to follow, much to be proud of.

COMPANIONSHIP

During his Wisdom Years, Adams had the blessing of companionship—some that came his way, and which he responded to with an open heart, some that resulted from his reaching out.

For decades, he had enjoyed the love, friendship, and often long-distance partnership of one of the most extraordinary women of his day. Now together at Quincy, they had family to celebrate, tragedies to grieve, love to share. From time to time children and grandchildren were taken into their home, sharing in the daily routines, the bountiful food, the happy conversations.

Their daughter-in-law Louisa Catherine would say that in Abigail's letters "the full benevolence of an exceptional heart and the strength of her reasoning capacity" were found. "We see her ever as the guiding planet around which all revolved performing their separate duties only by the impulse of her magnetic power."[18]

Through the years an assortment of non-family visitors stopped by—some for a meal or a conversation, some to stay under their roof for days. Visitors ranged from an occasional compatriot from revolutionary days to Massachusetts legislators to a West Point class of cadets to the young former class poet from Harvard, Ralph Waldo Emerson.

But in a way moderns can scarcely relate to, some of Adams most meaningful companionship resulted from the writing of letters.

Within the continental United States, mail delivery was agonizingly slow over the primitive roads of the day. Letters sent via sailing ships across the Atlantic could take weeks or months to deliver.

Nonetheless, they were the intellectual and emotional lifelines of the time, indispensable to Adams through much of his life, never more so than when he was physically isolated at Quincy.

For the first four years at Quincy, Adams made little effort to reach out beyond his family and neighbors. Then he decided to send a letter of greeting to his old friend and fellow signer of the Declaration of Independence, Benjamin Rush.

> Pray how do you do? How does that excellent lady, Mrs. R?...Is the present state of the national republic enough? Is virtue the principle of our government? Is honor? Or is ambition and avarice, adulation, baseness, covetousness, the thirst for riches, indifference concerning the means of rising and enriching, the contempt of principle the spirit of party and of faction the motive and principle that governs?[19]

Rush's reply was enthusiastic:

> My much respected and dear friend. Your letter of the 6th instantly revived a great many pleasant ideas in my mind. I have not forgotten—I cannot forget you....
>
> You and your excellent Mrs. Adams often compose a conversation by my fireside. We now and then meet with a traveler who has been at Quincy, from whom we hear with great pleasure not only that you enjoy good health, but retain your usual good spirits.[20]

Biographer David McCullough wrote how meaningful the letter-based companionship was to be to Adams:

> And so began an extended, vivid correspondence between the two men that was to occupy much of their time and bring each continuing enjoyment. For Adams it was as if he had found a vocation again. His letters to Rush became a great outpouring of ideas, innermost feelings, pungent asides, and opinions on all manner of things and mutual acquaintances—so much that he had kept within for too long...[21]

The resumption of correspondence with Benjamin Rush was one of the happiest events of Adams' life in retirement. Rush's wife remarked that the two elderly gentlemen were behaving like a couple of schoolgirls. And though they were never to see one another, the friendship grew stronger than ever.[22]

Among countless subjects, in one of his letters to Rush, Adams wondered why nations seemed to need war to bring forward their honor and integrity: "What horrid creatures we men are, that we cannot be virtuous without murdering one another?"[23]

Adams had selected in his correspondent a fitting match for his intellect and idealism, his desire to do good. Along with being a stalwart revolutionary, Rush was a leading medical doctor and a pioneer in treating mental disorders. In 1812 Rush sent Adams a first copy of *Medical Inquiries and Observations upon the Diseases of the Mind.*

"The subjects of them have hitherto been enveloped in mystery," he wrote to Adams. "I have endeavored to bring them down to the level of all other diseases of the human body, and to show that the mind and body are moved by the same causes and subject to the same laws." He expected to be attacked by the physicians of the day. "But time I hope will do my opinions justice. I believe them to be true and calculated to lessen some of the greatest evils of human life. If they are not, I shall console myself of having aimed well and erred honestly."[24]

The book was to become, for years, the standard guide for understanding and dealing with mental illnesses, and Rush would become known as the father of American psychology.

As an antecedent of modern psychology, Rush had a professional and personal interest in observing and drawing inferences from dreams. In a number of his letters to Adams, he had related several of his own dreams. Now he had a new one to report.

He dreamed that in the future he was studying American history, and he read of the renewal of friendship and correspondence between two former presidents, John Adams and Thomas Jefferson. According to the dream, it was Adams who rekindled the old friendship. Per Rush's dream:

> Mr. Adams addressed a short letter to his friend Mr. Jefferson in which he congratulated him upon his escape to the shades of retirement and domestic happiness, and concluded it with assurances of his regard and good wishes for his welfare. This letter did great honor to Mr. Adams. It discovered a magnanimity known only to great minds. Mr. Jefferson replied to this letter and reciprocated expressions of regard and esteem. These letters were followed by a correspondence of several years.[25]

Also, according to the dream, "these gentlemen sunk into the grave nearly at the same time."[26]

THE ADAMS JEFFERSON LETTERS

On New Year's Day, 1812, Adams made the first move. He took up his pen in his library and wrote a short letter to Jefferson quite like the one prophesized in Rush's dream. In the note Adams wrote that he would soon receive, by separate post, "a packet containing two pieces of homespun lately produced in this quarter by one who was honored in his youth with some of your attention and much of your kindness." He closed the letter, "I wish you sir many happy New Years…I am sir with a long and sincere esteem your friend and servant."[27]

The "homespun" that Adams was referring to was a copy of John Quincy's *Lectures on Rhetoric and Oratory* that he had authored as part of his professorship at Harvard.

Jefferson responded quickly and in kind:

> A letter from you calls up recollections very clear to my mind. It carries me back to the times when, beset with difficulties and dangers, we were fellow laborers in the same cause, struggling for what is most valuable to man, his right of self-government. Laboring always at the same oar, with some wave ever ahead threatening to overwhelm us and yet passing harmless under our bark, we knew not how, we rode through the storm with heart and hand, and made a happy port....I have heard with pleasure that you also retain good health, and a greater power of exercise in walking than I do...No circumstances have lessened the interest I feel in these particulars respecting yourself; none have suspended for one moment my sincere esteem for you; and I now salute you with unchanged affections and respect.[28]

Thus began what historian David McCullough called "one of the most extraordinary correspondences in American history—indeed, in the American language."[29]

This was to be John Adams crowning creative contribution of his Wisdom Years, a gift to future generations explaining from a unique vantage the world-changing experiment of the making of America.

Rush told Adams that he was overjoyed by the correspondence "which has taken place between you and your old friend Mr. Jefferson. I consider you and him as the North and South Poles of the American Revolution. Some talked, some wrote, and some fought to promote and establish it, but you and Mr. Jefferson *thought* for us all."³⁰

Within two years fifty letters traveled the rough roads between Quincy and Monticello, and this was just the beginning. Per McCullough in is definitive biography, *John Adams:*

> They wrote of old friends and their own friendship, of great causes past, common memories, books, politics, education, philosophy, religion, the French, the British, the French Revolution, American Indians, the American navy, their families, their health, slavery—eventually—and their considered views on life, society, and always, repeatedly, the American Revolution…
>
> They were two of the leading statesmen of their time, but also two of the finest writers, and they were showing what they could do.³¹

Adams' habits throughout his Wisdom Years made this extraordinary correspondence, this gift to history, possible: His regular exercise, his hearty companionship, his intellectual curiosity had kept him healthy, mentally sharp, emotionally engaged. His continuing broad reading provided a font of wisdom to draw upon. Indeed, he and Jefferson were among the most bookish exemplars of a bookish generation.

In their correspondence, Adams and Jefferson both postured that they ignored the politics of the day. "I have given up newspapers in exchange for Tacitus and Thucydides, for Newton and Euclid,"³² Jefferson said—while he was being kept well informed of the political scene by Madison and Monroe, as Adams was by John Quincy. Nonetheless, their shared focus on the big ideas of the classics and the Enlightenment rekindled their friendship and enriched their correspondence. And it provided the readers of their letters a treasure trove of understanding. Their correspondence is a window into the minds that *thought* for the Revolution.

While the two patriots agreed on much regarding what the idea of America was all about, they had their disagreements as well.

"Whether you or I were right posterity must judge," Adams wrote, explaining his thinking behind his views, trying to draw Jefferson out.

"Checks and balances, Jefferson, however you and your party may have ridiculed them, are our only security," Adams wrote. And, "What think you of terrorism, Mr. Jefferson?" And, "You and I ought not to die before we have explained ourselves to each other."[33]

The correspondence was an absolute joy to Adams during his Wisdom Years. Letters from Jefferson were eagerly anticipated, savored when received, read aloud at family gatherings.

While their philosophical wrangling engaged their minds, their expression of personal sentiments delighted their hearts.

After John Quincy Adams was elected president, Adams received warm congratulations from Monticello.

"It must excite ineffable feelings in the breast of a father to have lived to see a son to whose education and happiness his life has been so devoted so eminently distinguished by the voice of his country,"[34] Jefferson wrote.

"Every line from you exhilarates my spirits and gives me a glow of pleasure, but your kind congratulations are solid comfort to my heart,"[35] Adams responded.

Their correspondence continued through their long and full lives. Adams' passions and his prose remained vigorous to the end.

Among his last letters to Jefferson, Adams, a devout and faithful Christian, denounced the laws and practices of Europe and America which discouraged "free inquiry and private judgment," laws which made it "blasphemy to deny or to doubt the divine inspiration of all the books of the old and new Testaments from Genesis to Revelations... I think such laws a great embarrassment, great obstructions to the improvement of the human mind."[36]

JULY 4, 1826

In what was widely accepted as a sign of divine providence, and was certainly a testament to the strong wills of the two living lions of the American Revolution, John Adams and Thomas Jefferson died on the same day, as prophesied in Benjamin Rush's dream, remarkably, on July 4, 1826, the 50th anniversary of the signing of the Declaration of Independence.

Before he passed, hearing that it was the fourth of July, Adams said, "It is a great day. It is a good day."[37]

AUTHOR'S NOTES

● I have long admired the courage demonstrated by John Adams in defending the British soldiers involved in the so-called Boston Massacre. Adams demonstrated his patriotism and his sense of duty in countless ways throughout his service to his country. Adams and his fellow signers of the Declaration of Independence pledged "our lives, our fortunes, and our sacred honor" in support of their new country, the new idea of America. Those were literal risks for Adams, who put his family's well-being, and his own life, on the line many times in his years of service.

But it takes a special kind of courage to take a principled stand that seems at odds with the people you basically agree with, against the members of your own tribe to use Joseph Campbell's terminology. In defending the British soldiers,

Adams put at risk his friendships, his personal livelihood, and his reputation as a leader of the patriot cause to provide a fair and competent legal defense, to do the right thing.

How much we need that kind of courage and integrity today. John Adams serves as a compelling model for political and business leaders, and for each and every one of us in our day-to-day personal relationships. As Jesus said, we're prone to call out the speck in the eye of others and overlook the log in our own. Adams life reminds us to keep our own eye clear as well.

● Being rejected by his countrymen for his second term as President was a terrible emotional blow to Adams. Yet his priceless gift to history in co-authoring the Adams Jefferson letters is a powerful demonstration that we can creatively contribute during our Wisdom Years even following what may seem like a crushing defeat. Yet another demonstration of his courage and strength of heart.

● The lives we walk through in this book demonstrate that there is no single path to marital bliss. People can have happy, fulfilling, productive lives with multiple spouses engaged deeply in their life's work, or with a single partner whose life is mostly separate. I can personally attest that sharing meaningful work that you deeply care about with your soul-mate brings a special kind of joy. One can only wonder what kinds of contributions Abigail might have made in a society and in a time of equal rights for women. John and Abigail were truly blessed to have found each other in little Quincy. Their partnership is a blessing for us all.

Chapter Nine

MARTHA GRAHAM

Dance is the hidden language of the soul.

Martha Graham danced through the first act of her Wisdom Years.

She maintained a performance schedule that would have exhausted many younger dancers. When she was 73, on one of her many trips for the U.S. State Department as a good-will ambassador, Graham danced the lead role in *Clytemnestra*, in Lisbon, Portugal. She had recently created *Clytemnestra*, which was one of the first multi-hour modern dance performances. As had long been her custom, she designed the title role for herself to dance, one appropriate for her appearance and abilities in her Wisdom Years.

Graham choreographed the three-act, three-hour dance-drama so that she acted more than danced to conserve her energy through the long performances. Martha's was the title role, the aging queen of Greek mythology, "an angry wicked woman," who reviews her life to try to learn why she has been condemned to be amongst the dead in Hell. Her hands had been twisted into contorted claws by arthritis, and she made those hands part of her character's persona, dramatically thrusting them toward the audience from the front of the stage.

Graham's evil queen fascinated the audience, nowhere more than in the ancient bullring in Lisbon. The huge crowd cheered her on, shouting "*Ole! Ole!*"

Martha called that performance the culminating moment of her career. So far.

CHOSEN BY DANCE

The outline of Martha Graham's story would not make her an obvious choice to become American's leading practitioner of modern dance, the person most responsible for the form that it was to become. While many future dance performers begin their serious study by the time they are nine or ten, Martha began her first instruction when she was 22. Her instructor used words like homely, overweight, dumpy, and unprepossessing to describe his new student.

Despite her late start, Martha's early-life experiences, in hindsight, had provided the nourishment needed to help her find her life's passion. George Graham, her father, was a well-to-do family physician with a strong interest in psychology—he had once worked in a mental hospital. He told his young daughter something he learned from observing his patients: Movement never lies.

Martha and her two sisters grew up in the straight-laced Victorian age. Much of their day-to-day care was provided by Lizzie Prendergast, an Irish immigrant girl who served as the family's nanny, nurse, maid, and cook. Lizzie had never gone to school, but she loved the theater and attended plays on her days off. She liked to entertain the three Graham girls by singing songs from the popular musicals of the day.

The Graham girls had never been inside a real theater, but they made up plays of their own, with Lizzie's help. Their playroom became a make-believe theater, the girls wearing costumes that their mother had made for them. Martha installed a "curtain" across the room, a bed-sheet actually, and invited the whole family to attend a show she had made up. When the curtain was drawn back, Martha was revealed, singing her big number, a tune she had learned from Lizzie.

"I always wanted to go on the stage," she said as an adult. "I knew there was a magic someplace in the world that had to do with the stage."[1]

Lizzie often took Martha and her sisters with her to services at her Roman Catholic Church. Martha was enchanted by the lighted candles at the altar, the dramatic processionals, the statues of saints, the chanting, the ceremonies, the mystery. The sacred pageantry that she had been charmed by as a child would one day inform the dances she would create as an adult.

Martha's earliest years were spent in Allegheny in the heart of the Pennsylvania coal country, near the factories and steel mills of Pittsburgh. The air was black, the town was bleak, and everything was covered in coal dust. Not surprisingly, Martha's sister Mary suffered from asthma, and when Martha was fourteen Dr. Graham moved his family to Santa Barbara, California, a six-day journey by train. The sunny seacoast town, with its clear, fresh, ocean air, was a boon for Mary's health and a boon for Martha's spirit. The three girls loved playing on a flat-topped cliff overlooking the ocean. They would watch the waves crash into the shore far below, then run wildly across the plateau, arms spread wide, breathing in the sea air, their hair flying as they ran.

Martha thrived at Santa Barbara High School. She was a quick learner and an avid reader and became the editor of the school's literary magazine *Olive and Gold*. Her teachers recognized her gift for story-telling and for language, and they encouraged her as she wrote short stories and a two-scene play. She was an excellent athlete, enjoying basketball despite her short five-foot-two height. She took a sewing class and was soon able to cut and sew her own dresses.

One day Graham and her parents were walking down a Santa Barbara street when Martha saw a poster in a shop window that changed her life. The poster featured a bejeweled woman sitting on a throne-like platform, her lips hinting a smile. The photo was of the dancer Ruth St. Denis, dressed as Radha, the Hindu goddess. The poster was promoting her upcoming performances in nearby Los Angeles.

Martha was spellbound by the exotic poster and pleaded with her parents to let her attend one of the performances. Her father agreed, and he made the trip a special father-daughter event, buying her a new dress and giving her a corsage of violets.

Although Martha had never heard of her before seeing the poster, Ruth St. Denis was one of the great dancers of the time. Her performance at the Mason Opera House was a series of exotic dances inspired by the mysterious East. Martha was transfixed by St. Denis's expressive movements, as she could become one with burning incense, then portray cobras as her arms became coiling snakes, then transform herself into the Hindu goddess pictured on the poster. St. Denis communicated clearly without speaking, evoking the human pleasures of touch, smell, sound, taste, and sight through her movements.

"From that moment on," Graham recalled, "my fate was sealed. I couldn't wait to learn to dance as the goddess did."[2]

It was not an obvious career choice. In addition to her "advanced" age and her appearance, becoming a professional dancer was not deemed an acceptable career for a young lady of her station. Dr. Graham expected Martha to go to college, ideally to Vassar where his mother had studied, then marry well and raise a family.

In Martha's remaining two years of high school she dropped basketball to avoid injury to her legs and took up dramatics instead, earning leading roles in her junior and senior class plays. She joined the debating society and the drama club, and became the editor-in-chief of the graduation issue of *Olive and Gold*.

When she graduated from high school, she made it clear to her parents that she did not want to attend Vassar or any other such academic college. She had heard about the Cumnock School of Expression, an experimental junior college in Los Angeles where she could study both academic subjects and practical theater arts. By now her parents had learned that Martha quite had a mind of her own, and she successfully persuaded them to let her attend the school with a friend from Santa Barbara.

At Cumnock Martha took courses in art and literature, in acting, playwriting, and stage lighting. And she took a three-times-a week interpretive dance class.

After her three years at Cumnock, Martha auditioned at a new Los Angeles dance school that had been opened by her much-admired Ruth St. Denis and Ruth's dancer-husband Ted Shawn. It was called the Ruth St. Denis School of Dancing and Related Arts, better known as Denishawn

The audition was with Miss Ruth. A cigar-smoking pianist named Louis Horst played a waltz while Martha, terrified, moved about the room, impressing as best she could with what she had learned in her dance lessons at Cumnock. Miss Ruth didn't quite know what to do with Martha, and she assigned her to her husband Ted's class. He wasn't much impressed with Martha, but she was in, able to practice and study and learn and be near her idol.

Ruth St. Denis and another American, Isadora

Duncan, were creating a new kind of dance, distinct from classical ballet, ballroom dancing, or the popular soft shoe of vaudeville. They were among those leading dance into a new era, and they were coming to be recognized as serious artists.

St. Denis had started in vaudeville, but she wanted dance to be more. She was especially intrigued and inspired by the dancing forms and mysticism of India, Egypt, and the Far East. She favored a barefoot style and wanted her dance to capture the world of spirit.

Martha was fortunate to be in a unique place, one of the first professional schools of dance in the country. The teaching was informed by many influences, and the students learned Oriental dance, Spanish dance, American Indian dance, as well as basic ballet.

Denishawn students came from all over America. In addition to learning dance, they studied dramatic gesture, makeup, lighting, music, and costume design. They learned to think about dance deeply, studying its history and its philosophy. They discussed Oriental art and Greek philosophy, had sessions in yoga and meditation.

Despite her audition, Martha eventually impressed Miss Ruth with her mastery of the difficult steps and gestures, and with her raw talent and determination... so much so that Shawn created a new dance-drama with a starring role for her. *Xochitl* was the story of a beautiful Toltec maiden who dances fiercely to protect herself against the drunken advances of the emperor. Martha danced the role with such conviction that she brought her audiences to their feet. *Xochitl* became a huge success and by 1921 Martha was touring America as a featured soloist with the country's leading dance company.

Martha soon became manager of one of Denishawn's touring companies, in addition to being its star soloist. She was a temperamental perfectionist, wanting everything to go exactly right. During the cross-country tours, Martha spent hours and hours with Louis Horst, the company's music director. Horst was ten years older than Martha, and was separated from his wife. Along with being a musician, he was brilliant and literate, and had a deep appreciation of dancers. They became great lifelong friends.

"Louis brought me out," she recalled. "He saw me as something strange and different. He schooled me in certain behavior, discipline and a deep respect for music....He had the most to do with shaping my early life."[3]

The experience with Denishawn gave Martha unparalleled opportunities to grow and learn, but she soon became ready for a change. After seven years with the company, she broke away and moved to New York to become a featured soloist in the *Greenwich Village Follies*. Overnight Martha became a Broadway star, touring the country, performing in London, captivating audiences, earning a handsome salary.

After two seasons, at the age of 30, Martha left the *Follies*, ready to discover and to create her own form of dance.

REVEALING THE INNER WORLD, INVENTING MODERN DANCE

Modern dance, as it is now known, was largely shaped by what Martha Graham did with the next nearly 70 years of her life.

The Art Institute of Chicago had been a point of interest during one of her cross-country tours. There she had seen an abstract painting by the Russian artist Wassily Kandinsky—a slash of red running across a field of blue. It was one of the first modern paintings she had seen, and she had a visceral reaction. "I nearly fainted because at that moment I knew I was not mad, that others saw the world, saw art, the way I did....I said, 'I will do that someday. I will make a dance like that.' "[4]

Creating dance was her passion and her destiny, but Martha had to support herself. So she turned to teaching. She was named co-director of the newly formed dance department at the Eastman School of Music in Rochester, New York. There she would have a studio, students, and opportunities to choreograph. She taught three days per week at Eastman then commuted by train to New York City for her second job training performers for musical reviews. She also opened her own dance studio, a room at Carnegie Hall where she taught private lessons.

Graham selected three talented young women from among her students at Eastman to become her first dance group. She choreographed a program of eighteen short dances, designed and sewed the costumes with the help of her three dancers, and created the lighting effects. They borrowed a thousand dollars from a friend and "Martha Graham and Dance Group" rented a Broadway theater for one evening and made its debut. Despite the snowy night, the group attracted a big-enough audience to pay the theater and her debt.

The dances were evocative of the Denishawn days, and there was enough freshness to draw some positive comments from newspaper critics. "Decorative, pretty, undisturbing, and exotically graceful" give you a sense of their reactions, and the performance. Ever the self-critic, Graham later described those early dances as "childish things, dreadful."[5]

The authentic Martha Graham, the person so moved by the Kandinsky painting, slowly began to come forward in her new dances. During the next four years she created 79 new dances for herself and her Group, dances that broke new ground.

A striking example was Martha's first protest dance, *Revolt*, a portrayal of the outraged human spirit's reaction to injustice. It was shortly followed by *Immigrant* and the antiwar *Poems of 1917*. *Adolescence* explored the joys and needs of a young girl.

Her biographer Russell Freedman said,

> Martha was learning to express deep-seated feelings and strong convictions through the dynamic language of dance. Her classes became experimental laboratories where she began to develop a radically new way of dancing…[6]
>
> The 1920s were a decade of experimentation in all the arts—in painting, music, literature, and the theater—and this new breed of young dancers wanted to speak for the changing times in which they lived… Martha Graham and her fellow dance pioneers were ready to discard all the old rules. They wanted to create a new kind of dance, a uniquely American dance that would capture the spirit and energy of their country and their times.[7]

Martha and her dancers were dirt poor, doing work they loved. During the day the dancers worked as waitresses, sales clerks, and secretaries, so long as they could take part in the evening rehearsals that sometimes ran to one or two in the morning. The dancers were paid little, and that only for performances, nothing for rehearsals. For them dancing was not a "job," it was a cause, their life's calling. Martha made extraordinary demands on her students, sometimes terrifying them. But they admired her, even worshiped her. "Everybody was hypnotized, absolutely magnetized by Martha," one student recalled. "She opened our eyes to the arts. I was on fire."[8]

Martha herself made her own clothes and became

a vegetarian to save money on food. She was poor, doing what she loved.

Instead of the fanciful stories that were the stuff of classical ballet, Martha's dances explored themes of the daily lives of ordinary people. They danced on bare stages in simple outfits that the dancers had sewn themselves. Rather than ballet's graceful moves, their intention was to challenge the audience with stern facial expressions, blunt gestures, and spare movements. They sought to bring out and lay bare basic human feelings.

While Graham didn't care for the phrase "modern dance" (she preferred "contemporary dance" but didn't make an issue of it) that's how it came to be known because it addressed modern concerns.

In 1929 Martha Graham and Dance Group premiered *Heretic*, now regarded as her first major work. It nicely portrayed how Martha thought of herself at the time, how she felt about her work. In the starring role, Martha was dressed in white, her hair flowing. She danced in opposition to a double row of women in black Puritan-like dresses, their hair drawn back, their faces stern. Time after time the white-clad heretic tries to break through the barrier formed by the rows of women in black, but each time they act in unison to block her, stamping their bare feet on the floor. Some lunge at and spit on the heretic, while others turn their backs. In the end the heretic sinks to the floor, her spirit broken, defeated.

The dance was seen as a protest against intolerance, against condemning people simply because they are different. John Martin, the *New York Times* dance critic, said the performance was "strikingly original and glowing with vitality…[9] Audiences who come to be amused and entertained will go away disappointed, for Miss Graham's programs are alive with passion and protest. She does the unforgiveable thing for a dancer to do—she makes you think."[10]

Graham's work was all about connecting people with the inner world of emotions and feelings and dreams. To do that, she built a whole new vocabulary of movements. To express sadness or despair, she did not simply bow her head; her whole body would sink downward, often to the floor. She wanted to show on the outside what was going on in the inside. Her goal was for her dances to reveal the inner passions and the inner conflicts—the "interior landscape" we all share.

Lamentation, which Graham created in 1930, may have been her most haunting dance. Dressed in a mummy-like shroud with only her face, hands, and bare feet showing, she rocked with anguish from side to side, writhing as if trying to break free, a picture of deep, deep sorrow. Russell Freedman described her approach: "She did not dance *about* grief...but sought 'the thing itself'—the very embodiment of grief."[11]

Graham's success in portraying the inner world was unmistakable when after one performance a woman in the audience came to see Martha backstage. Through her sobs and her flowing tears the woman told Graham that her son had been struck and killed by a car several months earlier and she had been unable to express her grief until she saw *Lamentation*. Finally crying her tears, she let herself mourn in Martha's arms.

With its roots perhaps in Ruth St. Denis's teaching, Martha was fascinated by the dance of traditional cultures, both their diversity and their universal themes. She was deeply influenced by a trip she took in 1930 with Louis Horst to New Mexico. She was captivated by the ceremonial dances and the religious rituals they observed, a rich blend of Native American, Christian, and Spanish cultures. When she returned to New York she launched into the creation of *Primitive Mysteries*, her tribute to a Native American-

Hispanic ritual honoring the Virgin Mary.

After a year's hard work and lots of Martha's self-doubt, *Primitive Mysteries* opened in 1931 at the Craig Theater in New York. Dressed in white, Graham danced with a chorus of twelve women wearing dark blue. Louis's score for flute, oboe, and piano contained Native American themes, while the simple, intense dance captured the adulation of an ancient religious ritual.

The *New York Herald-Tribune* critic declared *Primitive Mysteries* "The most significant choreography which has yet come out of America...it achieves a mood which actually lifts both spectators and dancers to the rarefied heights of spiritual ecstasy."[12]

Graham pioneered in so many ways. For one, hers were the first dance performances to reverse the way dances had been put to music. Pre-Graham, dances were performed to flow with pre-existing musical compositions. Louis Horst inverted the traditional practice, beginning with *Fragments*, composing the music after Graham had choreographed the dance. It's a practice now commonplace in the movies, for example, where the music is composed to reinforce the mood that the director wants for the film, created or completed following the film editing.

One of her more enduring dance and musical collaborations was with Aaron Copland who composed the music for Graham's *Appalachian Spring*. The performance was a tribute to Martha's heritage, set in young America, in the region where she spent her earliest years, the home of her Puritan ancestors. The set was a minimalist representation of an Appalachian pioneer homestead, and the dance depicted a spring celebration as a bride and groom move into their newly built farmhouse.

Appalachian Spring premiered at a Library of Congress concert. Despite being 50 at the time,

Graham portrayed the young bride and Erick Hawkins danced the role of her young husband-farmer. One character played a pioneer woman modeled on Graham's great-grandmother, a beautiful, quiet woman. As the work ends, the newlyweds are left alone in their farmhouse, proud and strong and looking forward to raising a family.

Appalachian Spring was a huge success and Copland received a Pulitzer Prize for his musical score. The dance itself would become Graham's best-known work, and she would continue to perform the role of the "young bride" well into her sixties.

"Nothing Martha Graham has done before has had such deep joy about it," wrote John Martin, who said that Martha danced "like a sixteen-year-old."[13]

Graham pioneered in other ways as well. Long before the civil rights movement, hers was the first major dance company to include Asian and black dancers, and later the first to include men.

Her high ethical standards were a matter-of-fact part of her life. She turned down an invitation from the government of Nazi Germany to perform at the International Dance Festival, part of the 1936 Olympic Games. She would have gained worldwide publicity and likely substantial financial support as the United States representative. She just said no. "It never entered my mind even for a second to say yes," she said. "How could I dance in Nazi Germany?"[14]

"I would find it impossible to dance in Germany at the present time," she wrote to Joseph Goebbels, the German propaganda minister. "So many artists whom I respect and admire have been persecuted, have been deprived of the right to work for ridiculous and unsatisfactory reasons, that I should consider it impossible to identify myself, by accepting your invitation, with the regime that has made such things possible. In addition, some of my concert group (which included several Jews) would not be welcomed in Germany."[15]

After World War II Graham was told that her name was on a list of those to be "taken care of" when the Nazis controlled America.

"I took it as a great compliment,"[16] she said.

THE PROCESS OF CREATION

Just as Frederick Law Olmsted understood and taught that "everything matters" in a landscape, everything you see and smell and hear and feel, Martha Graham knew that everything matters in a dance performance.

The physicality of the dancers was a basic tool of expression, and she drilled her dancers for hours every day, a demanding routine of stretching, movement, and breathing exercise that they liked to call "the torture." The strength and flexibility of the back and leg muscles received her special focus, as well as the expressiveness of the dancers' movements. She drove herself most of all, often shutting the studio door and working by herself.

"Movement in modern dance is the product not of invention but of discovery—discovery of what the body will do,"[17] she said..

Along with music, costuming and makeup and lighting and staging received her intense attention; they were important arenas of experimentation. In the late 1920s and early 1930s, both her creative vision and her tight budget called for simplicity. Simple, unadorned costumes that the dancers made themselves were the rule, as well as white makeup and a gash of red lips. Later, after her costuming would become somewhat more elaborate, Graham jokingly referred to this time as "my period of long woolens."

Story was vital. Martha searched far and wide for

ideas. She studied psychology and Greek myths, read poetry and history and the Bible, practiced yoga and observed as she traveled. She was highly influenced by the ceremonies of traditional cultures, especially those of the American Southwest and of Mexico. She proudly stole ideas, and liked to steal from the best—Plato or Picasso if she could. Above all, she wanted to grow, to keep her ideas relevant and fresh and vibrant.

HER WISDOM YEARS—ACT I

Martha Graham's Wisdom Years were a remarkable performance, in two acts.

As she moved into her Wisdom Years, she was a one-of-a-kind cultural resource for the U.S. State Department. Audiences in Europe, Asia, and the Middle East flocked to see America's most famous modern dancer, the first to travel abroad as a cultural ambassador.

One trip for Martha and her company lasted four months and included visits to major cities in Israel, Iran, Japan, the Philippines, Thailand, Indonesia, Burma, and India. While the younger dancers in her group were ready to wilt from heat and exhaustion, Graham never missed a performance, dancing in each program, and giving lectures and interviews at each stop.

Audiences in Asia had never seen such so-called modern dances, but they were very understandable to them: They dealt with the eternal struggle of good versus evil, with gods and mortals, with the mysteries and the joys of the human heart—the stuff of their own traditions, the universal experience.

State Department officials said that Graham was the most effective ambassador they ever sent to Asia.

Between Martha's 65th and 75th years she continued to dance, creating ten new roles for herself, and eight other new dances for her company in which she did not appear. Of course she couldn't move as fast or kick as high as she once had, but she continued to dance.

Her *Acrobats of God* was a tribute to dancers, and a spoof in which she poked fun at modern dance, at classical ballet, at her own pretentions. *Phaedra* caused a hue and cry when it was performed as part of the American government's cultural exchange program. Two members of Congress, perhaps unaware of the Greek legend that inspired Graham's version of Phaedra, walked out of the performance and denounced it as shockingly erotic. "We couldn't quite make it out," said one Congressman, "but the import was clear."[18] If they had known the ancient legend, or stayed to the end of the performance, they would have seen that it delivers a stern warning when the wayward, lustful princess receives her punishment. The publicity made *Phaedra* a box-office hit, but audiences expecting lewd sexuality were disappointed: *Phaedra* was a serious work of art, an exploration of human passions.

Martha was still the featured star when she performed, but the roles she created for herself highlighted her acting gifts and were much less physically demanding than they had been decades before. She frequently used the flashback technique, for example allowing "the young Judith" or whomever to dance while Martha stood grandly at the edge of the stage watching her youthful self dance the hard stuff.

During these early Wisdom Years, Graham's company was performing at its peak: "All of them, men and women, are beautiful to look at; all of them are trained to the state of ease in energy; all of them have an underlying dramatic awareness of what is going on about them; and all of them move as if they were sentient branches of Martha Graham herself," wrote John Martin.[19]

Martha was immensely proud of her well-trained dancers, and worked hard to keep them at their best. She continued to be a relentless taskmistress.

Her life was full and her schedule was packed, but Graham was aware of her waning powers. Her arthritis continued to worsen, and when it flared up she moved with great pain. She wore long white gloves to hide her twisted hands. Angered by the reality of her aging body, she began to drink heavily. Finally, in 1969, Martha gave her last performance at the age of 75.

After retiring from dancing, Martha became deeply depressed. "I had lost my will to live," she wrote. "I stayed home alone, ate very little, and drank too much and brooded. Finally my system just gave in."[20]

Gravely ill, Graham was in and out of the hospital and mostly bedridden at home. She was not expected to recover.

"Without dancing, I wished to die," she said.[21]

But in the greatest creative act of her life, at the age of 78, three years after her last dance performance, Martha announced that she would again become the director of her company. After passing through the depth of her "black despair," she had discovered that only death itself could kill her urge to create.

HER WISDOM YEARS—ACT II

After she had resumed her duties as her school's chief director, after her 80th birthday, Graham led her dancers on an extended tour of Asia. With her on the tour was a young protégé, Ronald Protas, who would be second in command at the company, and eventually take over as artistic director.

Martha, vigorous in her 80s, wanted new projects, new dancers, new ideas. She taught classes almost daily, reconstructed some of her older works, and choreographed new works. After her 1973 return to choreography, Graham created more than twenty new works and thirty major revivals. Students came from all over the world to study with her.

In 1976 she received the Presidential Medal of Freedom, America's highest civilian honor, from President Gerald R. Ford. At the White House ceremony, President Ford, whose wife Betty had studied with Graham, called her "a national treasure."

Martha joined her company at the close of each performance, proudly taking center stage, and she continued to appear onstage in popular lecture-demonstrations. She was a striking figure with a gaunt face, a seductive voice, a faultless sense of timing, and colorful dresses. "I am elderly," she said, "and if I dress my age I will look older than God's aunt…so I choose to be flamboyant."[22]

The *Maple Leaf Rag*, Graham's last complete work, composed when she was 96, is one of her most joyful. A self-mocking commentary on her own legend, its musical score consists of the rag-time tunes of Scott Joplin, the music that Louis Horst had used to cheer her up more than 50 years before. It begins with a recording of Martha saying, "Oh, Louis, play me the 'Maple Leaf Rag.'"[23]

In the fall of 1990, when she was 96, she went with her company on a 55-day tour of the Far East. Back in New York, she came down with pneumonia. She never recovered, dying at home a few weeks before her 97th birthday.

Martha was choreographing and creating until the end, doing what she loved. But first and foremost, she wanted to be known as a dancer.

"Many people have asked me if I have a favorite role," she had said. "To which I always answer that my favorite role is the one I am dancing now."[24]

AUTHOR'S NOTES

● Martha's life is yet another tribute to the people who encourage and support childhood enthusiasms: parents, grandparents or teachers, friends or caregivers—the nanny in her case. Cultivating childhood enthusiasms often enough leads to lifetimes full of joy and wonder.

● The physical challenges of our bodies are real enough, but how we react is what counts. If Martha Graham could dance through arthritis until she was 75, who am I to complain about my aches and pains?

● Through her whole life, Martha chose to ignore or resist the prejudices of the day. Even though her actions put her success at risk, she simply chose to do what she felt was the right thing. What prejudices, blatant or subtle, do we confront in our lives? Do we say the thing or take the action that feels in accordance with our beliefs? It is a choice available to us all.

● Creating and contributing during our Wisdom Years, even in the field of one's life-long career, doesn't necessarily mean doing it in the same way as when we were younger. Graham danced until she was 75, but the dances she choreographed for herself in her Wisdom Years were much simpler and less physical then the ones of her earlier years. After her dancing ended, she created and contributed by choreographing dances for others, and by teaching. Contributing is not an all-or-nothing deal: Often one must find a new way. If Martha had given up because she could no long dance, the world would have missed out on some incredible choreography. If we get stuck on "I must do it the way I once did it—or not at all," we may miss valuable new ways to contribute.

● The big things are sometimes the simple ones. Find what you care about, and do it.

Chapter Ten

NELSON MANDELA

You encourage people by seeing good in them.

At the age of 76, Nelson Mandela was elected President of the Union of South Africa, the first black African elected to the presidency since the nation's formation in 1910.

Mandela had been released from prison just four years before—after spending *27 years* as a political prisoner, 18 of those years in a seven-by-eight-foot cell with a straw mat, three thread-bare blankets, and a 40-watt light bulb that burned all night.

Before being sent to prison, he had been a firebrand revolutionary, bitterly opposed to the nation's apartheid laws and determined to overthrow them, by violence if necessary. He had helped form the African National Congress's military organization—Umkhonto we Sizwe (MK), or "Spear of the Nation"—and had agreed to become the organization's Commander-in-Chief. The role meant that Mandela would become a fugitive, a professional revolutionary. He had thrown himself into the job with enthusiasm, voraciously reading histories of war and revolution, seeking money and military training from African countries that had successfully fought off their European colonial masters. The role had earned him a life sentence for sabotage.

Now, just four years out after decades of prison, he was elected to lead his nation.

After being freed from prison he and his African National Congress (ANC) colleagues had negotiated with the ruling minority Afrikaners a revised constitution which would allow all adults to vote for the first time, not just the white minority. Nelson's vision was of a peaceful, prosperous, multi-racial society, one which respected the rights of each individual—the majority African natives and all minorities. His negotiations with the Afrikaners called for their continuing participation in the new government, presuming it would be led by the black majority.

After decades of revolution and decades of prison, Mandela averted civil war and led his nation to reconciliation.

"People are human beings, produced by the society in which they live," Mandela said. "You encourage people by seeing good in them."[1]

He was a role model to his nation and to the world—during his Wisdom Years.

APARTHEID

Today it's difficult to imagine the humiliating realities of the institutionalized discrimination that was the law of South Africa under apartheid just a few decades ago. Each person was classified by race, different races were required to live in different parts of the cities, and mixed marriages were prohibited. Bars, busses, and beaches were officially segregated. "For Use By White Persons Only" was a common sign in public places.

The Pass Law Act was especially hated by the black majority, the pass-books a despised symbol of apartheid. The law said that all black South Africans over the age of 16 must carry a pass-book at all times within white-designated areas. The pass-book documented permission requested and denied or granted to be in a certain area. Any white government employee could cancel the permission for a black to remain in an area. The law led to thousands of arrests, and riots that caused many deaths.

Peaceful efforts by the ANC and other groups to overturn these degrading laws were brutally resisted by the ruling National Party, and Mandela and the ANC turned to threats of violence and sabotage in an effort to force change by the government. The result was his arrest and conviction, at the age of 46, to a sentence of life in prison.

THE PRISON YEARS

Few people indeed would respond to 27 years in prison as did Nelson Mandela.

He went into prison with one important vision of leadership drawn from his guardian who had raised him following his father's death when Mandela was nine. His guardian, Jongintaba, was the local Regent, somewhere between the local king and tribal chief.

Growing up, he carefully observed the Regent's exercise of leadership in the tribal meetings. He remembered this experience later while he was in jail, when he wrote:

> One of the marks of a great chief is the ability to keep together all sections of his people, the traditionalists and reformers, conservatives and liberals, and on major questions there were sometimes sharp differences of opinion...the Regent was able to carry the whole community because the court was representative of all shades of opinion.[2]

Throughout his whole live, even in jail, Mandela carried in his head and in his heart an idealized image of tribal society. He described this image in a speech in 1962:

> Then our people lived peacefully, under the democratic rule of their kings and their *amapakati*, and moved freely and confidently up and down the country without let or hindrance. Then the country was ours, in our own name and right. We occupied the land, the forests, the rivers; we extracted the mineral wealth below the soil and all the riches of this beautiful country. We set up and operated our own government, we controlled our own armies and we organized our own trade and commerce.

In his eyes, the tribal council was the democratic ideal:

> The council was so completely democratic that all members of the tribe could participate in its deliberations. Chief and subject, warrior and medicine man, all took part and endeavored to influence its decisions. It was so weighty and influential a body that no step of any importance could ever be taken by the tribe without reference to it.[3]

Now in prison on Robben Island, as a result of isolation from the world, his agreements and disagreements with his fellow prisoners and his jailers, and his off-and-on opportunity to read and to learn, Mandela thought more deeply than ever about his principles and his ideas. He harnessed and directed his strong will; he learned to empathize and persuade, to control his temper, to project his authority.

A newcomer prisoner on Robben Island was astonished to meet the Mandela who he had known only as a revolutionary. He explained how the "new" Mandela affected him: "I came out a different person: totally philosophical about things...What amazed me about Nelson and Sisulu and other people who had life sentences was the calmness, the equanimity with which they led their lives. They didn't throw in the towel. They didn't display bitterness. They showed me how to laugh at the tortures we went through."[4]

Mandela's personal growth was not the result of elegant surroundings or enlightened warders, as the prison guards were called. For three years the prisoners were required to wear degrading khaki shorts—the uniform of "native boys." They had no access to newspapers or radio. At first they could only write and receive one letter every six months, and no letter was to be more than five hundred words. Real news about what was going on in the country was strictly censored.

The warders were typically uneducated Afrikaners; many were orphans, some were brutal.

As part of their punishment, the prisoners' routines were intentionally harsh: At 5:30 each morning they were woken to clean their cells and wash in cold water in an iron bucket. They were given nearly inedible breakfasts of corn porridge in the prison's stark courtyard. Until midwinter they worked in the courtyard mindlessly hammering stones into gravel. As one inspector wrote in his report, it was a punishment which could "drive the most phlegmatic man into a state of fury....To have to sit in the sun without moving and without being allowed to speak to one's neighbor was hell on earth."[5] The political prisoners were only allowed to talk with each other briefly when they washed, or took their meals, or worked in the hell-hole of a lime quarry, the center of Mandela's daily life for several years.

Mandela hoped his living conditions might improve if he could impress the warders, even make friends with them, with a combination of respect and assertiveness. He learned the very human truth that the warders were not all evil, that they were individuals, and that in fact many could be changed.

"I soon realized that when an Afrikaner changes he changes completely and becomes a real friend,"[6] he later said. He explained the ANC's policies to young warders and to visiting prison officials at every opportunity. In the process, he developed his persuasion skills with this key segment of South African society.

The former hothead also learned to keep his cool. He demonstrated the ability to restrain himself in the face of provocations—to the amazement of his fellow prisoners who had seen him so often lose his temper in the past. He regarded the warders with pity rather than hatred, and he could see that their personal fears and insecurities were the basis of their brutality.

Mandela developed a far-reaching interest in Afrikaners, reading many Afrikaans books, and learned to speak the language reasonably well. He urged his fellow political prisoners to try to understand their mindset.

"I realized the importance of learning Afrikaans history, of reading Afrikaans literature, of trying to understand these ordinary men…how they are indoctrinated, how they react," said one prisoner. "They all have a blank wall in their minds. They just could not see the black man as a human being.…You must understand the mind of the opposing commander… you can't understand him unless you understand his literature and his language."[7]

Simple human connections had practical benefits. Mandela found that "an ordinary warder, not a sergeant, could be more important to us than the

Commissioner of Prisons or even the Minister of Justice...when you had a good relationship with the warders in your section it became difficult for the higher-ups to treat you roughly."[8]

Often his reaction was that of simple human kindness, such as when he encouraged his fellow prisoners to teach the illiterate warders to read, or help them with their legal problems.

After his contacts with warders, Mandela emphasized to his compatriots the value of reaching out to liberal Afrikaners. In a 1977 paper he anticipated the opportunity that would present itself in 15 years:

> Afrikaner politicians have no monopoly of their people just as we have none over ours. We ought to speak directly to the Afrikaner and fully explain our position. Honest men are to be found on both sides of the colour line and the Afrikaner is no exception. We have a strong case and the Afrikaner leaders will command undivided support only as long as their people are ignorant of the issues at stake...
>
> A violent clash is now unavoidable and when we have fought it out and reduced this country to ashes it will be necessary for us to sit down together and talk about the problems of reconstruction—the black man and the white man, the African and the Afrikaner.[9]

In prison Mandela and his ANC friends also developed their skills in urging moderation to the other political extreme.

In the later 1970s, violent young black activists joined them in prison. They had heard the message of American black revolutionaries such as the Black Panthers and had swallowed it whole. The new prisoners were angry, angry young men.

Mandela set out to convert these radicals to the more moderate policies of the ANC. To do so, he pursued the soft approach of gentle persuasion.

As one prisoner explained: "One by one, the ANC underground on Robben Island worked on us—on individuals—talking with us and smuggling notes to us."

"It was amazing to us that in spite of so many years on the island they were still so courageous, mentally alert and determined to fight on," said another. "We developed a deep comradeship with them through discussions and understanding of the problems we face in South Africa. We also felt great respect. They were like fathers to us."

A third said: "How I changed! All because I met Nelson Mandela and learned from him and the others....It was then that I began to question some of my Black Consciousness beliefs, because here was our leader preaching unity and non-racialism."[10]

COMPANIONSHIP AND LEARNING

Mandela's personal growth flourished in prison for a reason. His extraordinary spirit was nurtured by several factors, including the companionship of some of his closest friends, and a passionate commitment to a lifetime of learning.

Prison officials allowed him to continue his correspondence studies for his Bachelor of Law degree at London University. A table and chair was added to his cell.

Fortunately for Mandela, the government decided to incarcerate all of the political prisoners at Robben Island, the better to keep their eye on them and prevent them from influencing others. The decision was a god-send for the dissidents as it made it possible for rival parties to find common ground. The prison became a years-long political workshop.

Mandela continually fostered discussion and debate between the different political parties. People who had previously been bitter enemies developed a shared understanding of their common goals, and a common vision of a multi-racial democracy.

"We couldn't see a future—it was blank," one prisoner said. "But Mandela always could."

He taught songs and poems, such as the Victorian poem "Invictus," by W.E. Henley:

Out of the night that covers me,
Black as the Pit from pole to pole,
I thank whatever gods may be
For my unconquerable soul...

It matters not how strait the gate,
How charged with punishments the scroll,
I am the master of my fate;
I am the captain of my soul.[11]

"When you read words of that nature you become encouraged," Mandela later said. "It puts life in you." [12]

Together, Mandela and many of his fellow prisoners found an amazing capacity for forgiveness; they were resolved to avoid self-pity.

Mostly educated in British schools, they shared a common culture in their appreciation of the works of Shakespeare. Shakespeare always had something to say to them; his understanding of suffering and courage and sacrifice reminded the prisoners that they were part of the human experience. They would recite long passages from Shakespeare, and debate their meaning.

One prisoner kept a disguised copy of Shakespeare's works on his shelf, and he circulated it to all of the prisoners, inviting them to mark their favorite passages. Mandela's favorite was from *Julius Caesar*:

> *Cowards die many times before their deaths;*
> *The valiant never taste of death but once.*

Perhaps the most remarkable aspect of the prisoners' determination to control their own emotional and mental fates was their commitment to formal education within the Robben Island prison. This is how the prisoners' resolve was described by biographer Anthony Sampson in *Mandela: The Authorized Biography:*

> It was the opportunity to study that was most precious to the prisoners. Mandela had earlier urged the Commissioner to "let the atmosphere of a university prevail," and by the late sixties that atmosphere was appearing: The quarry was becoming a kind of campus for what came to be called "the university of Robben Island." ….Anyone with a degree or other qualification would teach his subject, and each morning they would plan their courses at the quarry. They would combine teaching even with hard labor…
>
> Mandela taught a course on political economy, tracing the development of societies from feudalism to capitalism to socialism—which he still saw as the most advanced stage. But he preferred arguing to teaching, and always welcomed questions from his pupils, which forced him to think harder about his views. He saw the Robben Island system as essentially Socratic, using dialogue to clarify the ideas of both teachers and pupils.[13]

Some of the prisoners were illiterate when they arrived, and before long they were enthusiastically learning to read and write. Many progressed to formal correspondence studies, acquiring the opportunity for higher education they might never have had otherwise. Some young warders picked up the education bug as well; the news had spread and many warder recruits volunteered for Robben Island.

The reality of prison life, with its total lack of distractions, provided a unique opportunity for focused study. The dearth of textbooks put a premium on memory; prisoners could later recount passages they had heard years before.

This atmosphere had a profound effect on Mandela. It sharpened his already exceptional memory, and his mind was disciplined by argument. And he was deepening his intellectual interests and his appreciation of ideas.

Beyond the formal studies, Mandela just loved to read, which he did voraciously, devouring the books he was able to get his hands on in prison. He enjoyed Steinbeck's *The Grapes of Wrath* and the great Russian writers; he read War and Peace in three days. While he read Afrikaans writers, he mostly read in English. He read Dickens, Wordsworth, Tennyson, and Shelley. He especially enjoyed political biographies such as Kennedy, Lincoln, Washington, Disraeli, and Churchill. He loved Churchill's style, his cadence, the music of his words.

"From year to year he was changing and revising his views," said a fellow prisoner. "He didn't have ideological depth before he came in: He got that in prison."[14]

NATURE

During his many years in prison, Mandela's spirit was also nurtured by his connections with nature—few and far between though they may have been, he savored each one. He often said he was "just a country boy," and the tiniest connection with the natural world seemed to rekindle in him warm emotional memories of the Transkei countryside of his youth.

Mandela sought out or created nature connections whenever he could. At Robben Island he actually preferred being at the lime quarry—hard work and extreme heat and all—to the stale prison courtyard. In the quarry there was open air and glimpses of nature.

After Red Cross reports had criticized the conditions of the political prisoners, their work in the quarry was alternated with collecting seaweed which would be sold as fertilizer. The work was hard there as well, and the ocean icy-cold in winter, but Mandela savored the view of the ocean, the antics of the swooping seabirds, the unspoiled natural beauty of the island. The prisoners made lunch of mussels and clams, and caught abalone and crayfish for seafood stew which was shared by prisoners and warders.

Mandela's happiest times in Robben Island came when prison officials allowed the prisoners to plant a small garden in a corner of the courtyard. The rocks were cleared from the soil, seeds were obtained from the warders, rows of vegetables were carefully laid out and planted.

"Nowadays the garden is Nelson's baby and he is fanatical about it," wrote one of the prisoners. "As expected he has read everything he could lay his hands on."[15]

To enrich the soil they collected the bones after any meal with meat and hammered them into powder. Within a year they had raised onions, sweet melons, watermelons, nearly a thousand tomatoes, and two thousand chilies.

Mandela thought of the garden as a metaphor for politics. A leader, he wrote, "sows seeds, and then watches, cultivates and harvests the result."[16]

In 1982 Mandela and three other prisoners, after being on Robben Island for 18 years, were suddenly moved to the Pollsmoor prison in a leafy Cape Town suburb. Even though the neighborhood was full of gardens and vineyards, and the building looked cheerful from the outside, inside it was a dark world of corridors and rows and rows of barred cells. There were 15 locked doors between his cell and the outside world.

Happily, Mandela quickly became on friendly terms with the prison commander who made it possible for him to make a garden on the roof. The commander provided 16 oil drums, cut in half and filled with good soil. Mandela spent a couple of hours on his little farm every day, eventually growing 900 vegetable plants including carrots and broccoli.

"He has a sort of obsession with his garden," one of his colleagues wrote. "You can't imagine the amount of time and energy which he expends on his plants."[17] Mandela called it his "garden in the sky."

Of course far more than the plants were being nurtured. Mandela was nurturing his soul, building up his reservoirs of strength, preparing himself for his role to come in leading his nation.

THE INTERNATIONAL COMMUNITY

It's difficult to exaggerate the role of pressure from the international community in bringing about the end to apartheid. Decisions and actions from the private sector, from governments, and from nonprofit organizations all played a role.

Amnesty International brought to public light the government's complacency about massacres of Africans. Red Cross reports brought pressure for improved prison conditions.

International sanctions of the apartheid regime were extremely important. During the Cold War, the attention of the United States and other western powers waxed and waned depending on local politics: Every decision seemed to be screened through the question of how best to fight "the Red Menace." Life and death questions, issues of human rights and morality, were secondary.

Presidents George H.W. Bush and Bill Clinton were personally supportive of Mandela and his peaceful revolution. The Black Caucus in Congress mobilized its political clout. Ronald Reagan and Margaret Thatcher, however, were on the wrong side of history, resisting sanctions to the end.

Under the strong pressure of international sanctions, and with growing violent protests, the investment community contributed the fatal blow to the apartheid regime. Chase Manhattan Bank stopped rolling over its loans, other banks withdrew credit, pension funds withdrew their investments, the country's currency value fell, and the South African Reserve Bank had to obtain loans at much higher rates from German and Swiss banks.

Many foreign bankers decided they would not invest in South Africa under apartheid. The government was becoming unmanageable, the country ungovernable.

To many, including the apartheid government, the solution became clear. The world's most famous prisoner would need to be released.

NEGOTIATIONS

In 1990, Nelson Mandela was released from prison. He was 72.

To old friends he seemed much changed from 30 years before. Gone were his aggressiveness and arrogance and defensiveness; he was a gentle man with a warm smile. He was emotionally released from the bitterness of the past, focused on creating a better future.

Mandela seemed acutely aware of his icon status; he was determined to be the role model for his nation. He exuded a quiet dignity; he understood that he was always on stage, always the personification of his cause, always the moral leader.

"I'm just a sinner who keeps on trying," he said. "I am not particularly religious or spiritual. I am just an ordinary person trying to make sense of the mysteries of life."[18]

As a political leader, he had a unique advantage. He hadn't clawed and compromised his way to the top. It appeared that he had parachuted into his leadership role with his principles intact.

Not long after his release, the ANC and Afrikaner government teams began preliminary talks as a prelude to formal negotiations. Mandela showed himself to be a more moderate leader than his young ANC comrades had expected, not the revolutionary head of a guerrilla army who had been jailed years before.

The ANC, for example, had long championed nationalization of the country's large businesses as a way to address the extreme economic inequalities within their society. But shortly upon his release from prison, Mandela developed a different view. At the World Economic Forum in Davos, Switzerland—where Mandela was celebrated as a hero by the world's business establishment—he argued at first that other industrialized countries such as England, Japan, and Germany had required nationalized industries to restore their economies after world wars. He made the case that the war that had been waged against his people had been just as injurious.

However Mandela listened thoughtfully as others argued against this view. The world has changed, he was told; it's now a global economy. No nation can develop its economy separate from other nations. Leaders from former communist countries told him how they had embraced free enterprise as the Soviet Union collapsed.

"They changed my views altogether," Mandela summed up later. "I came home to say: 'Chaps, we have to choose. We either keep nationalization and get no investment, or we modify our own attitude and get investment.' "[19] Well into his Wisdom Years, Mandela was more than willing to embrace a new way of thinking if it furthered his ultimate goals.

One of the first important political actions Mandela took after Davos was to take part in negotiations between the ANC and the existing South African government. Mandela and F.W. de Klerk, president of South Africa at the time, both understood that peaceful talks were their only practical way forward. Neither side could force their will on the other through armed conflict without a frightening loss of life.

Mandela saw that he faced the greatest challenge of his whole life—negotiating a peaceful solution without a violent response from either the black revolutionaries or the white conservatives. De Klerk had to keep his diehards and generals on board; Mandela had to placate the angry firebrands.

The parties adopted a Declaration of Intent, "to bring about an undivided South Africa, with one nation sharing a common citizenship, patriotism and loyalty."[20]

This peaceful way of negotiating was not typical of how other disputes were being addressed at the time. Disagreements in Northern Ireland, Yugoslavia, and the Middle East resulted in armed conflicts and death, while South Africa hosted one of the most famous negotiations in history.

Mandela's was a delicate balancing act. He continually reminded de Klerk of his global clout and he maintained the threat of mass mobilization and armed struggle...while he cultivated personal trust with his opponents.

During the negotiations, Mandela displayed nerves of steel. "He can be very brutal in a calm and collected sort of way," a negotiating partner said afterward. "He sets his mind on doing something and he becomes unshakable. We would never have been able to negotiate the end of apartheid without Mandela."[21]

Mandela embraced a huge compromise that was the key to a democratic settlement. Revolutions have been described as the kicking in of a rotten door. The trick is to put something better in place—a system that works, a system that lasts—following the revolution.

That understanding was what made America's founders, and their legacy of a democratic nation, so extraordinary. Binding the nation's wounds, avoiding a continuing insurrection in the South, consumed President Lincoln's attention toward the end of the Civil War, and was his enduring accomplishment.

Nelson Mandela recognized that need in the Union of South Africa. He knew that the prospect of a prosperous, peaceful nation required a sense of ownership by all segments of society, including the minority whites.

He and the ANC agreed to safeguard the jobs of white civil servants and provide for a coalition government of Afrikaner Nationalist and ANC ministries. It was agreed that elections would be followed by a five year government of national unity which would include all parties polling over 5 percent of the votes cast.

In the midst of the negotiations a tragedy threatened the whole process. Chris Hani, perhaps the nation's second most popular black leader, was shot and killed by a white assassin. Fortunately, an Afrikaner woman saw the assassin's license-plate number and immediately contacted the police. Fifteen minutes later the assassin, a Polish immigrant, was stopped by police, literally with the smoking gun.

De Klerk issued a statement of condolence, but he recognized that it was up to Mandela to calm the people. Mandela flew to the scene to make one of the most important speeches of his life. It began:

> A white man, full of prejudice and hate, came to our country and committed a deed so foul that our whole nation now teeters on the brink of disaster. A white woman, of Afrikaner origin, risked her life so that we may know, and bring to justice, this assassin.[22]

There was some rioting and violence following the shooting, but there was no bloodbath. Mandela's statesmanlike speech, and the public's calm response, suggested that he was already the leader of the country.

Peace was maintained, negotiations continued, and the nation was on its way to its first multi-racial elections. In 1993, de Klerk and Mandela were named joint winners of the Nobel Peace Prize.

LEADING THE NATION

> *History says don't hope*
> *On this side of the grave.*
> *But then, once in a lifetime*
> *The longed for tidal wave*
> *Of justice can rise up,*
> *And hope and history rhyme.*[23]

The world was watching as elections were held in South Africa. An estimated 200,000 officials observed the voting by 23 million people.

The results came in with Mandela and the ANC winning 62.6% of the votes, a clear mandate but short of the two-thirds majority that would allow them to amend the constitution. Mandela understood that it was a blessing that the majority could not "do what they want." He well knew that the continuing participation of the Afrikaners in the government would be essential to transformation to a well-functioning multi-racial society.

The outgoing government organized a splendid inauguration ceremony in Pretoria. It was attended by thousands, including heads of state from throughout the world, and viewed by an estimated billion people on television.

In his speech Mandela stressed reconciliation:

> Out of the experience of an extraordinary human disaster that lasted too long must be born a society of which all humanity will be proud... Never, never and never again shall it be that this beautiful land will again experience the oppression of one by another, and suffer the indignity of being the skunk of the world.

The world was euphoric about the election. It was a fairy tale, a time of happy ever after.

But Mandela knew the simple reality. "We have no experience of elections, of parliamentary practice, and of state election,"[24] he said.

Looking back, he later said, "We were taken from the bush, or from underground outside the country, or from prisons, to come and take charge. We were suddenly thrown into this immense responsibility of running a highly developed country."[25]

An important element of his effectiveness was not Mandela's knowledge of the nuances of currency exchange rates or of the management of large bureaucracies; it was the simple, respectful way he related to people.

De Klerk was allowed to continue to live in the official presidential residence. Mandela knew the names of the people who worked for him, and their families—his security force, the gardeners, the women who brought him tea. He cultivated friendly relations with his Afrikaner security team members, who developed an intense loyalty to him. "I used to do it for the money, now it's for him," one of them said. "I'd take the bullet for him."[26]

His doctors said he had the energy of a man 20 years younger than his 76 years. He kept up his healthy habits, rising early in the morning most days to walk.

Mandela embraced his role as the father figure of the government, and of the nation. For all of his countrymen, he was the man of destiny.

He finessed the ANC with him as they transitioned from protest to governing.

Mandela's years of fostering open discussion and moving to consensus served him well as he presided over his Cabinet, a mixture of blacks and Afrikaners. The discussions were surprisingly nonpartisan, the Afrikaners sincerely committed to making the coalition work. ANC overall policies tended to be adopted, the Afrikaners usefully focused on the details of implementation.

"There was a boyish boarding school camaraderie which was very South African," one participant said. "Ninety-nine percent of the discussion was unideological…you couldn't tell they came from different parties."[27]

Cabinet members of all points of view just set down together to address the nation's problems.

Mandela gave a lot of responsibility to his protégé First Deputy President, Thabo Mbeki, a former exile. Mbeki took turns presiding over the cabinet with Second Deputy President de Klerk. It was a remarkable tribute to Mandela's leadership, and to the new spirit of the country, that the two deputies—formerly bitter enemies—worked together effectively to set agendas and assist in directing the Cabinet, and to manage the government.

Mandela left much of the details of running the government to Mbeki while he concerned himself with the broader issue of transforming South Africa from a white oligarchy into a healthy multi-racial society.

A new constitution was slowly negotiated to replace the interim one. It contained compromises all around, including providing safeguards for Afrikaners' culture and language. As a testimony to the challenge of the process and the wisdom of the compromises, pretty much everyone criticized it, and all subsequently endorsed it.

Difficult financial conditions were faced, challenging decisions made. Much needed to be fixed. The National Party had run up huge deficits and overmanned nationalized industries. Its leaders were notorious for taking bribes. Now other nations and global financial institutions were urging the ANC to shed government jobs, privatize industries, and rapidly reduce the deficit.

While Mandela was immensely popular at first, the honeymoon was soon over as difficult decisions were made to govern responsibly.

He learned a nuanced leadership approach: "In nation building you sometimes need a bulldozer, and sometimes a feather duster,"[28] he said.

One immensely popular move Mandela made was to actively support and identify with South Africa's rugby team, the Springboks. The story was dramatized by the Hollywood motion picture, *Invictus*, directed by Clint Eastwood. Mandela championed the mostly white team in the mostly white sport, which many Africans thought symbolized the minority's arrogance. In 1995 the Springboks dramatically reentered the international rugby world with a World Cup win against New Zealand. The match was played in Johannesburg, and Mandela presented the trophy to the Springbok captain, Francois Pienaar, as the Afrikaner crowd wildly chanted, "Nel-son! Nel-son!" The win brought the nation together as nothing had, and won Mandela the hearts of millions of rugby fans.

Governing, and helping the nation heal, were consuming jobs for Mandela during his Wisdom Years.

Healing did not mean forgetting. One of the government's most controversial actions was setting up the Truth and Reconciliation Commission. The commission, which was headed by Archbishop Desmond Tutu, granted amnesties if the perpetrators revealed the truth and could prove that their actions had been politically motivated. Mandela promised that the commission would be free of political pressures.

In its five-volume report, strong accusations were made against both members of the National Party and the ANC.

Mandela was firm in his belief in both facing up to the truth, and in forgiveness: "We must regard the healing of the South African nation as a process, not an event."[29]

WITHDRAWING GRACEFULLY

Committed to a single term as President, Mandela always behaved more like a beloved monarch than an executive president, and he increasingly focused on unifying his people, taking the long view. When de Klerk left the government in 1996, Mandela expressed his gratitude for helping to avoid a bloody civil war.

"You mustn't compromise your principles, but you mustn't humiliate the opposition," he said. "No one is more dangerous than one who is humiliated."

While he was in office, he began the transition. He knew he could not be perceived to be the "indispensable man."

"Thabo Mbeki is already de facto President of the country. I am pushing everything to him," Mandela said on television. "My stepping down will be very smooth."[30]

He emphasized the same theme in his speech to his final ANC conference:

> More often than not an epoch creates and nurtures the individuals who are associated with its twists and turns: and so a name becomes the symbol of an era. As we hand over the baton it is appropriate that I should thank the ANC for shaping me as such a symbol of what it stands for...
>
> We take leave so that the competent generation of lawyers, computer experts, economists, financiers, doctors, industrialists, engineers and above all ordinary workers and peasants can take the ANC into the new millennium. I look forward to that period when I will be able to wake up with the sun, to walk the hills and valleys of my country village, Qunu, in peace and tranquility.[31]

As Mandela eased into peace and tranquility in his personal life, he did so in a very public way.

Not long after being released from prison, Mandela had obtained a divorce from his wife Winnie. During his prison years, Winnie had been the public face of the Mandelas, the strident protester, the person who kept the name in the global media.

Upon his release, it became obvious to Nelson that Winnie was more in love with the spotlight than with him. She refused to embrace reconciliation, continued to turn to violence, and seemed a little crazy. A very public, very painful, divorce ensued.

Six months after his release, Mandela visited Mozambique where he first met Graca Machel, the widow of the former president. Their friendship grew to love, and they married on the day before his 80th birthday. Two thousand guests joined the birthday party, helping to celebrate the happy ending to his remarkable public career, and the happy beginning of his married life with Graca.

President Clinton's moving tribute celebrated Mandela's marriage, and his life's work:

> In every gnarly, knotted, distorted situation in the world where people are kept from becoming the best they can be, there is an apartheid of the heart. And if we really honor this stunning sacrifice of twenty-seven years, if we really rejoice in the infinite justice of this man happily married in the autumn of his life, if we really are seeking some driven wisdom from the power of his example, it will be to do whatever we can, however we can, wherever we can, to take the apartheid out of our own and others' hearts.[32]

AUTHOR'S NOTES

● *Who we vote for, the companies we give our business to, the nonprofit organizations that we support, matters. In the United States and throughout the developed world, most people give little thought to the influence we might have on the lives* of people far away. We want to pay attention, to make our decisions with intention. What products we buy, and who earns our vote, might mean life or death to people on the edge in the developing world.

● We've discussed the lesson from Deepak Chopra: Firmly establish your intention, hold the vision of your goal, but be flexible as you go, alert to new ways of thinking, to what the world serves up for you if you pay attention. As one of many examples, if Mandela had clung to the ANC's original notion of nationalizing the country's major industries, his government, his fundamental goals, may well have failed.

● Again, nature. How very important early and continuing connections with nature can be to people's lives. In Mandela's case, his life work was not directly related to environmental stewardship, as was the case with Olmsted and Maathai. Nor did nature directly inform his creative output, as was the case with Georgia O'Keeffe. But connections with nature—as a child, and especially amongst the most trying conditions in prison as an adult—fueled his soul. Nature seemed to have been an important factor in the strength of heart he displayed as a leader, especially during his Wisdom Years.

● When one learns of this man's responsibilities, his energy, his schedule, his accomplishments after returning to freedom, you have to keep reminding yourself that he was 72 when he was released from prison. What a tribute to the possibilities during our Wisdom Years!

Final Thoughts

CREATING AND CONTRIBUTING DURING THE WISDOM YEARS

You do not know the road ahead of you:
You are committing your life to a way.
— *Ralph Waldo Emerson*

In the prologue, I said that I selected the people for this book because they made creative contributions during their Wisdom Years in diverse arenas that I care about—improving the environment, fostering personal and spiritual development, and building a well-functioning society.

Upon reflection, despite their differences, there is a fundamental factor that they have in common: They each said yes to the journey, to the prospect of a larger life—and they never turned back, especially during their Wisdom Years.

In *The Hero with a Thousand Faces*, Joseph Campbell described the archetypical hero's journey. It begins with the call to a higher purpose, a summons to leave the well-known past and journey into the grand unknown, into new ways of being. Those who make the journey persist through all manner of distractions and risks, through countless setbacks.

The lives that we have reviewed reveal a mixture of the attitudes and actions that are possibilities for most of us during our Wisdom Years:

- They stayed engaged, focused on the future, and created strong connections with people they cared about.

- They maintained healthy habits, mostly.
- They persevered though setbacks, including serious health issues, seeing them as episodes to move through rather than reasons to be disengaged from life.
- They expressed the courage of their convictions—rejecting discrimination, going against the grain when it was the right thing to do.
- They mentored young people, passing along their wisdom, and giving future generations the space to flourish.

No matter what the reality of our lives, those are choices available to most of us.

Their lives also show things available to us to champion—opportunities that we can help create for our children and grandchildren—and needs to champion in society.

- They had rich childhood experiences. Their parents did not push them toward their life pursuits—their lives were seldom what might have been envisioned by their parents—but their early lives helped support the creation of a "sense of wonder," a sense of the possibilities, that enflamed their spirits. Georgia O'Keeffe's mother's attitude was the extreme, but not a bad model. She made sure that Georgia and her sisters had music and art lessons, that they had the things about the house that the girls could use to explore their passions—then she left it to them to make of them what they will. Oh, and she hung Georgia's paintings around the house, her silent statement that she cared.

These people had a sense of being connected with the natural world and with the rest of humanity. Many especially related to traditional cultures, studied them and learned from them. They had a spirit of inclusion, be it with peoples far away, or individuals who were victims of prejudice in their own lives.

There is one special factor that links these people, and others who make their Wisdom Years their best: They were people of hope. They took their dreams seriously, and often their dreams came true.

It's never too late: How can you respond to the call to a larger life?

END NOTES

Chapter 1: Frederick Law Olmsted

[1] Stevenson, Elizabeth. *Park Maker: A Life of Frederick Law Olmsted*. New York: Macmillan Publishing Co., Inc., 1977, p. 155.
[2] Olmsted to Parke Godwin, August 1, 1958. *The Papers of Frederick Law Olmsted, Volume III*, p. 3.
[3] Stevenson, Elizabeth. *Park Maker: A Life of Frederick Law Olmsted*. New York: Macmillan Publishing Co., Inc., 1977, p. 260.
[4] Ibid., p. 271.
[5] Hines, Thomas S. *Burnham of Chicago*. Chicago: University of Chicago Press, 1979, p. 114.
[6] Stevenson, Elizabeth. *Park Maker: A Life of Frederick Law Olmsted*. New York: Macmillan Publishing Co., Inc., 1977, p. 389.
[7] Frederick Law Olmsted Papers, Manuscript Division, Library of Congress, Washington, D.C., November 3, 1891.
[8] Pinchot, Gifford. *Breaking New Ground*. New York: Harcourt, Brace and Company, 1947, pp. 48-49.

Chapter 2: Georgia O'Keeffe

[1] Eldredge, Charles C. *Georgia O'Keffe*. New York: Harry N. Abrams, Inc., 1991, p. 143.
[2] Ibid.
[3] Ibid., p. 21.
[4] Karbo, Karen. *How Georgia Became O'Keeffe: Lessons on the Art of Living*. Guilford, Ct.: Globe Pequot Press, 2012, p. 30.
[5] Ibid., p. 63.
[6] Ibid., p. 64.
[7] *Lovingly, Georgia: The Complete Correspondence of Georgia O'Keeffe & Anita Pollitzer*, p. 40.
[8] Eldredge, p. 20.
[9] Ibid.
[10] Karbo, p. 89, p. 96.
[11] Eldredge, p. 75.
[12] Ibid., p. 78.
[13] Ibid., p. 85.

[14] Karbo, p. 115.
[15] Ibid.
[16] Eldredge, p. 82, 83.
[17] Ibid., p. 94.
[18] Ibid., p. 95.
[19] Georgia O'Keeffe to Catherine O'Keeffe Klenert, July 1929. Estate of Catherine O'Keeffe Klenert.
[20] Eldredge, p. 112.
[21] Ibid., p. 119.
[22] Karbo, p. 217

Chapter 3: Joseph Campbell
[1] Campbell, Joseph with Moyers, Bill. *The Power of Myth*. New York: Anchor Books, 1991, p. xvi.
[2] Ibid., p. 26.
[3] Ibid.
[4] Ibid., p. 228.
[5] Ibid., p. 229.
[6] Ibid., p. 100.
[7] Ibid., p. 99.

Chapter 4: Carl Jung
[1] Jeffrey, Scott. *Creativity Revealed: Discovering the Source of Inspiration*. Kingston, New York: Creative Crayon Publishers, 2008, p. 24.
[2] Campbell, Joseph with Moyers, Bill. *The Power of Myth*. New York: Anchor Books, 1991, p. 61.
[3] Ibid., p.51.
[4] Chopra, Deepak. *The Spontaneous Fulfillment of Desire: Harnessing the Infinite Power of Coincidence*. New York: Harmony Books, 2003, p. 75.
[5] Jeffrey, pp.147,148.
[6] Jung, Carl. *Memories, Dreams, Reflections*. London: Routledge & Kegan Paul, 1963, p. 58.
[7] Stevens, Anthony. *Jung*. New York: Sterling Publishing Co., Inc., 1994, p. 8.

⁸ Stevens, p. 16.
⁹ Wikipedia.org/Cetonia aurata
¹⁰ Chopra, p. 60.
¹¹ Ibid., p. 119.
¹² Jung. *Memories, Dreams, Reflections*. p. 118.
¹³ Ibid., p. 124.
¹⁴ Stevens, p. 158.
¹⁵ Stevens, Preface.
¹⁶ Jung. *Memories, Dreams, Reflections*. p. 172.

Chapter 5: Wangari Maathai
¹ Maathai, Wangari. *Unbowed: A Memoir*. New York: Alfred A. Knopf, 2006, p. 4.
² Ibid., p. 52.
³ Ibid., p. 46.
⁴ Ibid., p. 125.
⁵ Ibid., p. 134.
⁶ Ibid., p. 135.
⁷ Ibid., p. 137.
⁸ Ibid.
⁹ Gore, Al. *Earth in the Balance: Ecology and the Human Spirit*. New York: Houghton Mifflin Company, 1992, p. 287.
¹⁰ Maathai, p. 175.
¹¹ Ibid., p. 293.
¹² nobelprize.org
¹³ unep.org

Chapter 6: Walt and Roy Disney
¹ Flower, Joe. *Prince of the Magic Kingdom: Michael Eisner and the Re-Making of Disney*. USA: John Wiley and Sons, Inc,, 1991, p. 11.
² Ibid., p. 12.
³ Ibid., p.14.
⁴ Pinsky, Mark I. *The Gospel according to Disney: Faith, Trust, and Pixie Dust*. Louisville, Kentucky: Westminster John Knox Press, 2004, p. xi.

[5] Flower, p. 24.
[6] Watts, Steven. *The Magic Kingdom: Walt Disney and the American Way of Life*. New York: Houghton Mifflin Company, 1997, p. 422.
[7] Ibid., p. 427.
[8] Ibid., p. 434
[9] Ibid.
[10] Thomas, Bob. *Building a Company: Roy O. Disney and the Creation of an Entertainment Empire*. New York: Hyperion, 1998, p. 307.
[11] Ibid., p. 311.
[12] Ibid., p. 316.
[13] Watts, p. 17.
[14] Marling, Karal Ann. *Designing Disney's Theme Parks: The Architecture of Reassurance*. Paris: Flammarion, 1997, p. 156.
[15] Ibid., p. 170.
[16] Watts, p. 435.
[17] Ibid., p. 436.
[18] Ibid., p. 437.
[19] Ibid, p. 440.
[20] Ibid., p. 439.

Chapter 7: Margaret Mead

[1] Howard, Jane. *Margaret Mead: A Life*. New York: Ballantine Books, 1984, p. 52.
[2] Boas, Franz. T*he Mind of Primitive Man*. New York: Macmillan, 1946 (orig. publ. 1911).
[3] *American Journal of Sociology* 31:5 (March 1926), p. 667.
[4] Mead, Margaret. "Social Organization of Manu'a," *Bernice P. Bishop Museum Bulletin 76* (Honolulu, Hawaii, 1930; reissued 1969), p. 476.
[5] Mead, Margaret. *Letters from the Field 1925-1965*. New York: Harper and Row, 1977, p. 19.
[6] Mead, Margaret. *Coming of Age in Samoa: A Psychological Study of Primitive Youth for Western Civilization*. New York: William Morrow, 1961 (orig. publ. 1928), p. 270.
[7] Ibid., Preface to the 1973 edition.
[8] Howard, Jane. pp. 85-86.

END NOTES

[9] Mead, Margaret. *Coming of Age in Samoa*. Preface to the 1973 edition.
[10] Letter from William Morrow, June 20, 1928, Library of Congress.
[11] Howard, Jane. p. 111.
[12] Koffka, Kurt. *The Growth of the Mind: An Introduction to Child Psychology*. New York: Harcourt Brace and Company, 1924.
[13] Mead, Margaret. *Growing Up in New Guinea: A Comparative Study of Primitive Education*. New York: William Morrow, 1975 (orig. publ. 1930), p. 19.
[14] Mead, Margaret. *Letters from the Field*, p. 135.
[15] Mead, Margaret. *Sex and Temperament in Three Primitive Societies*. New York: William Morrow, 1963 (orig. publ. 1935).
[16] Ibid., p. 259.
[17] Ibid., p. 282.
[18] Ibid., p. 322.
[19] Ibid.
[20] Mead, Margaret. Letter to John Dollard, September 23, 1936.
[21] Mead, Margaret; Bateson, Gregory. *Balinese Character: A Photographic Analysis*. New York Academy of Sciences, 1962, p. 5.
[22] Mead, Margaret. *Sex and Temperament in Three Primitive Societies*, p. 280.
[23] Howard, Jane. p. 205.
[24] Mead, Margaret. *And Keep Your Powder Dry*. New York: William Morrow, 1975 (orig. publ. 1942).
[25] Ibid., p. 183.
[26] Howard, Jane. p. 374.
[27] Ibid., p. 351.
[28] Ibid., p.385.
[29] Ibid., p.386.
[30] Ibid., p.391.
[31] Ibid., p.236.

Chapter 8: John Adams
[1] Butterfield, L. H., ed. *Diary and Autobiography of John Adams*, I, p. 352.
[2] Wroth, L. Kinvin and Zobel, Hiller B., eds. *Legal Papers of John Adams*. Cambridge, Mass.: Harvard University Press, 1965, III, p.

242.
3 Ibid., p. 269.
4 Ibid., p. 266.
5 Abbott, W.W.; Chase, Philander D.; Twohig, Dorothy, eds. *The Papers of George Washington, III,* p. 389.
6 McCullough, David. *John Adams.* New York: Simon & Schuster, 2001, p. 532.
7 Mitchell, Stewart, ed. *New Letters of Abigail Adams,* ****p. 220.
8 McCullough, p. 551.
9 Brown, R.A. *Presidency of John Adams.* Lawrence: University of Kansas, 1975, p.174.
10 McCullough, p. 566.
11 John Adams to Cotton Tufts, Dec. 26, 1800, Adams Papers, Massachusetts Historical Society.
12 John Adams to Colonel Joseph Ward, Feb. 4, 1801, Adams Papers, Massachusetts Historical Society.
13 McCullough, p. 571.
14 Ibid., p. 629.
15 Ibid., p. 630.
16 John Adams to Mr. DeWint, March 3, 1820, Adams Papers, Massachusetts Historical Society.
17 McCullough, p. 569.
18 Ibid., p. 625.
19 Ibid., p. 588.
20 Butterfield, L.H.,ed., *Letters of Benjamin Rush,* Vol. I-II, Princeton, N.J.: American Philosophical Society, 1951, p. 890.
21 McCullough, p. 589.
22 Ibid., p. 594.
23 *Old Family Letters Copied from the Originals for Alexander Biddle.* Philadelphia: Lippincott, 1892, p. 224.
24 Butterfield, p. 1164.
25 McCullough, p. 600.
26 Cappon, Lester J., ed. *The Adams-Jefferson Letters.* Chapel Hill: University of North Carolina Press, 1917, p. 285.
27 Ibid., p. 290.
28 Ibid., p. 291.
29 McCullough, p. 605.
30 Butterfield, p. 1127.

[31] McCullough, p. 605.
[32] Cappon, p. 291.
[33] McCullough, p. 607.
[34] Cappon, p. 609.
[35] Ibid.
[36] Cappon, p. 608.
[37] McCullough, p. 646.

Chapter 9: Martha Graham

[1] Martha Graham: *The Dancer Revealed*, PBS video documentary, 1994.
[2] McDonagh, Don. *Martha Graham: A Biography*. New York: Praeger, 1973, p. 16.
[3] Kisselgoff, Anna. "Martha Graham." The New York Times Magazine, February 19, 1984, p. 54.
[4] Graham, Martha. *Blood Memory*. New York: Doubleday, 1991, p. 98.
[5] McDonagh, Don, p. 50.
[6] Freedman, Russell. *Martha Graham: A Dancer's Life*. New York: Clarion Books, 1998, p. 44.
[7] Ibid., p. 47.
[8] DeMille, Agnea. *Martha: The Life and Work of Martha Graham*. New York: Random House, 1991, p. 130.
[9] Ibid., p. 89.
[10] Armitage, Merle, Ed. *Martha Graham*. Brooklyn, N.Y.: Dance Horizons, 1996, p. 8.
[11] Freedman, Russell, p. 61.
[12] Gardner, Howard. *Creating Minds: An Anatomy of Creativity Seen Through the Lives of Freud, Einstein, Picasso, Stravinsky, Eliot, Graham, and Gandhi*. New York: Basic Books, 1993, p. 282.
[13] DeMille, Agnea, p. 261.
[14] Graham, Martha, p. 151.
[15] McDonagh, Don, p. 113.
[16] Ibid., p. 151.
[17] Stodelle, Ernestine. *Deep Song: The Dance Story of Martha Graham*. New York: Schirmer Books, 1984, p. 56.
[18] New York Times, September 10, 1963.

[19] Stodelle, Ernestine, p. 128.
[20] Graham, Martha, p. 237.
[21] Ibid., p. 238.
[22] DeMille, Agnea, p. 421.
[23] Freedman, Russell, p. 146.
[24] Graham, Martha, p. 255.

Chapter 10: Nelson Mandela

[1] Sampson, Anthony. *Mandela: The Authorized Biography*. New York: Vintage Books, 1999, p. 12.
[2] Mandela, Nelson. Jail Memoir (unpublished), 1975-76.
[3] Mandela, Nelson. *The Struggle Is My Life*. London: International Defense and Aid Fund for Southern Africa, 1978, p. 141.
[4] Sampson, Anthony. pp. 226-227.
[5] Alexander, Neville. *Robben Island Dossier 1964-1974*. Cape Town: UCT Press, 1994, p. 32.
[6] Sampson, Anthony. p.214.
[7] Bernstein, Hilda. "Two South Africans from the Island," The Times, Jan. 18, 1978.
[8] Sampson, Anthony. p.214.
[9] Mandela, Nelson. "National Liberation" (unpublished essay), 1977.
[10] Sampson, Anthony. p.274.
[11] Henley, W.E. "Invictus." 1875.
[12] Sampson, Anthony. p. 212.
[13] Ibid., pp. 233-234.
[14] Ibid., pp. 236.
[15] Ibid., p. 232.
[16] Mandela, Nelson. *Long Walk to Freedom* (revised edition). London: Abacus, 1995, p. 583.
[17] Sampson, Anthony. p. 321.
[18] Ottaway, David. *Chained Together: Mandela, de Klerk and the Struggle to Remake South Africa*. New York: Time Books, 1993, p. 50.
[19] Sampson, Anthony. p. 429
[20] Ibid., p. 451.
[21] Ibid., pp. 457-458.
[22] Ibid., p. 461.

END NOTES

[23] Heaney, Seamus. "Doubletake" from *The Cure at Troy*. 1990.
[24] Mandela, Nelson. *Nelson Mandela Speaks: Forging a Democratic, Nonracial South Africa*. Johannesburg: David Philip, 1994, p. 252.
[25] Star & S.A. Times, April 1, 1998.
[26] Sampson, Anthony. p. 489.
[27] Ibid., p. 501.
[28] Ibid., p. 512.
[29] Ibid., p. 524.
[30] Ibid., p. 532.
[31] Ibid., p. 535.
[32] Clinton, Bill. White House speech. Sept. 22, 1998.

ACKNOWLEDGEMENTS

I am deeply grateful to my wife Nancy Rosenow for her inspiration, insightful editing, patience, and loving encouragement at every stage of the creation of this book. And to Stacy Hadley for her superb design of the cover and page layout.

I am grateful to Drs. Ron and Mary Hulnick, who lead the University of Santa Monica, for providing such marvelous models of creating and contributing during their Wisdom Years. And to Christina, Dario, Kathy, Brian, and Steve for their support through the long process of researching, writing, and editing the book.

I am grateful to the people I have written about, and to so many, many others, who show us the way for living long and full lives, rich with possibilities.

And I am so grateful to Nancy and our children and grandchildren—Stacy, Matt, Chris, Sylvie, and Lyla—who give me so much to look forward to as I move into my Wisdom Years. They are all the incentive I need to do whatever I can to leave the world a better place.